CONTEMPORARY
ISSUES
COMPANION

Genocide

Other Books of Related Interest:

Genocide

GREENHAVEN PRESS

An imprint of Thomson Gale, a part of The Thomson Corporation

Detroit • New York • San Francisco • New Haven, Conn. • Waterville, Maine • London

THOMSON

GALE

304.663 GEN 2007

Genocide.

Christine Nasso, *Publisher*
Elizabeth Des Chenes, *Managing Editor*

© 2007 Thomson Gale, a part of The Thomson Corporation.

Thomson and Star logo are trademarks and Gale and Greenhaven Press are registered trademarks used herein under license.

For more information, contact:
Greenhaven Press
27500 Drake Rd.
Farmington Hills, MI 48331-3535
Or you can visit our Internet site at http://www.gale.com

Articles in Greenhaven Press anthologies are often edited for length to meet page requirements. In addition, original titles of these works are changed to clearly present the main thesis and to explicitly indicate the author's opinion. Every effort is made to ensure that Greenhaven Press accurately reflects the original intent of the authors. Every effort has been made to trace the owners of copyrighted material.

Cover photograph reproduced by permission of

LIBRARY OF CONGRESS CATALOGING-IN-PUBLICATION DATA

Genocide /
      p. cm. -- (Contemporary issues companion)
   Includes bibliographical references and index.
   ISBN-13: 978-0-7377-3321-1 (hardcover)
   ISBN-13: 978-0-7377-3322-8 (pbk.)
   1. Genocide--Juvenile literature. 2. Genocide--History--20th century--Juvenile literature.
   HV6322.7.G445 2007
   304.6'63--dc22

                                                                            2007004506

ISBN-10: 0-7377-3321-7 (hardcover)
ISBN-10: 0-7377-3322-5 (pbk.)

Printed in the United States of America
10 9 8 7 6 5 4 3 2 1

Contents

Chapter 3: The Prevention of Genocide

Foreword

In the news, on the streets, and in neighborhoods, individuals are confronted with a variety of social problems. Such problems may affect people directly: A young woman may struggle with depression, suspect a friend of having bulimia, or watch a loved one battle cancer. And even the issues that do not directly affect her private life—such as religious cults, domestic violence, or legalized gambling—still impact the larger society in which she lives. Discovering and analyzing the complexities of issues that encompass communal and societal realms as well as the world of personal experience is a valuable educational goal in the modern world.

Effectively addressing social problems requires familiarity with a constantly changing stream of data. Becoming well informed about today's controversies is an intricate process that often involves reading myriad primary and secondary sources, analyzing political debates, weighing various experts' opinions—even listening to firsthand accounts of those directly affected by the issue. For students and general observers, this can be a daunting task because of the sheer volume of information available in books, periodicals, on the evening news, and on the Internet. Researching the consequences of legalized gambling, for example, might entail sifting through congressional testimony on gambling's societal effects, examining private studies on Indian gaming, perusing numerous Web sites devoted to Internet betting, and reading essays written by lottery winners as well as interviews with recovering compulsive gamblers. Obtaining valuable information can be time-consuming—since it often requires researchers to pore over numerous documents and commentaries before discovering a source relevant to their particular investigation.

Greenhaven's Contemporary Issues Companion series seeks to assist this process of research by providing readers with useful and pertinent information about today's complex issues. Each volume in this anthology series focuses on a topic of current interest, presenting informative and thought-provoking selections written from a wide variety of viewpoints. The readings selected by the editors include such diverse sources as personal accounts and case studies, pertinent factual and statistical articles, and relevant commentaries and over views. This diversity of sources and views, found in every Contemporary Issues Companion, offers readers a broad perspective in one convenient volume.

In addition, each title in the Contemporary Issues Companion series is designed especially for young adults. The selections included in every volume are chosen for their accessibility and are expertly edited in consideration of both the reading and comprehension levels of the audience. The structure of the anthologies also enhances accessibility. An introductory essay places each issue in context and provides helpful facts such as historical background or current statistics and legislation that pertain to the topic. The chapters that follow organize the material and focus on specific aspects of the book's topic. Every essay is introduced by a brief summary of its main points and biographical information about the author. These summaries aid in comprehension and can also serve to direct readers to material of immediate interest and need. Finally, a comprehensive index allows readers to efficiently scan and locate content.

The Contemporary Issues Companion series is an ideal launching point for research on a particular topic. Each anthology in the series is composed of readings taken from an extensive gamut of resources, including periodicals, newspapers, books, government documents, the publications of private and public organizations, and Internet Web sites. In these volumes, readers will find factual support suitable for use in reports, debates, speeches, and research papers. The anthologies also facilitate further research, featuring a book and periodical bibliography and a list of organizations to contact for additional information.

A perfect resource for both students and the general reader, Greenhaven's Contemporary Issues Companion series is sure to be a valued source of current, readable information on social problems that interest young adults. It is the editors' hope that readers will find the Contemporary Issues Companion series useful as a starting point to formulate their own opinions about and answers to the complex issues of the present day.

Introduction

The twentieth century witnessed more genocides than any other century thus far in recorded history. Beginning with the Armenian genocide in 1915, the world has seemed bent on its own self-destruction. Although many genocides occurred before the twentieth century, including, according to some sources, the American Indian genocide beginning in the 1400s and the Christian Crusades (1095–1291), the twentieth century was particularly bloody. Genocide expert R.J. Rummel of the University of Hawaii estimates that more than 262 million people were killed during the genocides of the twentieth century. The number and frequency of genocides during this time period is due in part to higher population density, mass media advances, and the disconnection between politicians and the people they govern. The 1994 Rwanda genocide, which resulted in the deaths of more than eight hundred thousand people, provides a powerful example of each of these circumstances.

As the world population increased, scarcity of resources led to conflicts. For example, in the years preceding the Rwanda genocide, regional and world economic and political changes contributed to a decrease in land, jobs, and food as the population soared. Before the genocide, Rwanda's population had exceeded 7.5 million, making it one of the most densely populated countries in Africa. Fear and despair about the future among Rwandan youth further contributed to the unrest that had spread throughout the citizenry as land was reassigned and food production fell.

Extremists played on the psychological distress of the already marginalized Hutu, convincing them that they had to kill their Tutsi neighbors in order to survive. Peter Uvin, professor at the Fletcher School of Law and Diplomacy at Tufts University in Boston, writes that "as Rwanda's experience shows, resource scarcity can be used as a political tool: Deliberate strategies to impoverish certain groups, to destroy food and livelihoods, and to promote fear were all built on this base." In other words, by inducing an "us" vs "them" way of thinking using resource scarcity, forces that were planning to take over the country were able to manipulate ordinary citizens into murdering their fellow countrymen.

In the past, leaders of genocidal movements had to rely on word-of-mouth to organize and carry out their vicious attacks. As technology rapidly advanced in the twentieth century, so did the ability to encourage others to engage in mass killing. Just as Hitler used the radio as a means to broadcast anti-Semitic propaganda, so did the Hutu leaders use the radio to broadcast anti-Tutsi dogma during the Rwanda genocide. In Rwanda, the local radio station, Radio Milles Collines, broadcast anti-Tutsi propaganda in the months leading up to the genocide. Later, broadcasters gave precise instructions on how to carry out the acts of genocide. In *Crimes of War*, Colette Braeckman notes that "when the killing was unleashed on April 6, [1994,] it became clear what the owners and managers of the station had created—an infernal pulpit from which the message to kill could be disseminated throughout Rwanda."

To even begin to comprehend the incredible power these radio broadcasts had on the Rwandan people, it is necessary to understand the important purpose radio serves in Rwanda and the rest of Africa. According to political science writer Dina Temple-Raston, "Radio is king. The first thing Africans buy when they get a job is a radio." Knowing the enormous amount of trust the Rwandan people had in radio broadcasters, the leaders of the genocide used it as a platform to express hate. The world recognized the intimate role radio played in the genocide and put several radio broadcasters on trial for genocide.

The growth of the world population and the rapid development of new technologies, like mass media, also contributed to the distance between government officials and the people they ruled. As human communities grew from villages to towns to cities, the need for centralized, depersonalized government grew. In the case of Rwanda, the country was colonized by the Germans in 1898 and then by the Belgians in 1923. Ruling from a distance, the Belgians felt that they had to develop an effective system to control the Rwandan people. They encouraged the Hutus to rise up against the Tutsis. They even instituted a countrywide identification card that clearly labeled each citizen according to his or her ethnic group.

In 1973, Juvenal Habyarimana overthrew the existing government. The battle between the Hutus and Tutsis continued. During Habayarimana's time in office, he instituted a number of measures that contributed to the discord between the Hutus and Tutsis, including mobilizing Hutus against the Rwandan Patriotic Front (RPF), a group of Tutsi refugees in Uganda who aimed to take back their country. According to the BBC News, "Habyarimana chose to exploit this threat as a way to bring dissident Hutus back to his side, and Tutsis inside Rwanda were accused of being RPF collaborators." After Habyarimana's death in a mysterious plane crash in 1994, genocide began.

Although high population density, advances in mass media, and distant governance are not the only reasons acts of genocide escalated in the twentieth century, certainly their contributions have been devastating. The authors in *Contemporary Issues Companion: Genocide* examine the issue of genocide in the following chapters: Defining Genocide, The Origins of Genocide, and The Prevention of Genocide. Choosing and presenting viewpoints on the subject of genocide is a difficult undertaking. The topics are sensitive by their very nature and can elicit strong emotional responses. Acts of genocide are almost always accompanied by attempts at denial.

Contemporary Issues Companion: Genocide endeavors to present the spectrum of opinions students can expect to be confronted with. Only by examining all sides of an issue is it possible to refute or champion any one viewpoint. While it is too soon to say if the world community will be successful in preventing the duplication of such mass atrocities as the twentieth century witnessed, perhaps the lessons learned from tragedies like the one in Rwanda will at least come to bear on how it responds to them.

CHAPTER 1

Defining Genocide

Genocide Is Difficult to Define

Jacques Semelin

Since Raphael Lemkin coined it in 1943 in response to the Armenian genocide, the term "genocide" has been a source of conflict. In the following viewpoint Jacques Semelin focuses on the limitations of the term as it is shaped by survivor memories, humanitarian action, legal issues, and revenge against enemies. He concludes that an accurate, universally accepted definition of genocide has not yet been determined. Semelin is a professor of political science at the Institut d'Études Politiques de Paris, where he teaches courses about genocide and international politics. He is the author of many articles and several books, including the forthcoming Purify and Destroy: The Political Uses Of Massacres and Genocides, *and encouraged the creation of the* Online Encyclopedia of Mass Violence.

Since the United Nations adopted the Convention on the Repression and Punishment of the Crime of Genocide on 9 December 1948, this word—genocide—has come to mean absolute evil, mass atrocities against defenceless civilians. Created in 1943 by the Polish jurist Raphael Lemkin, the term has known increasing international acceptance. Thus, one has talked about 'genocide' in almost every major deadly conflict of the second half of the twentieth century: from Cambodia to Chechnya, including Burundi, Rwanda, Guatemala, Colombia, Iraq, Bosnia, Ethiopia, the Sudan . . . and so on.

The term has also been used retrospectively to qualify the massacre of inhabitants of Melos by the Greeks (fifth century BC), of the Vendean people in 1793 by the French revolutionary army, the native people in North America, the Armenians in 1915, including the cases of famine in Ukraine, the various

Jacques Semelin, "What Is 'Genocide'?" *European Review of History*, vol. 12, no. 1, March 2005. © 2005 Taylor & Francis Group, Ltd. Reproduced by permission of Taylor & Francis Group, Ltd., www.tandf.co.uk/journals, and the author.

deportations of population in the Stalinian ex-USSR as well as, of course, the extermination of European Jews and gypsies but also the American nuclear bombings of Hiroshima and Nagasaki. This list is by no means exhaustive.

Applying this 'genocide' notion to these very heterogeneous historical situations raises many objections and passionate debates. These numerous 'handlings' of the concept express the need to resort to a word of universal significance to point out a major phenomenon in the twentieth century: that of the mass destruction of civilian populations. Other expressions have appeared, such as 'politicide', proposed by Ted Gurr and Barbara Harff, or 'democide' by Rudolf Rummel, but the word 'genocide' continues to dominate the field of social sciences, and it has given rise today to 'genocide studies'. The development of the new *Journal of Genocide Research* shows the dynamism of this field of study.

The Usages of an Ambiguous Word

The first problem arising from the word 'genocide' thus refers to its uses. It takes part in various kinds of political, identitarian or humanitarian rhetoric. This is a full-fledged matter of research whose several uses reveal some issues of great significance. First, *issues of memory*. When a population has been slaughtered, the survival community struggles so that this past suffering be recognized as genocide. The most emblematic struggle in this field is that of the Armenian community. Second, *issues of humanitarian action*, when NGOs [nongovernmental organizations] state that a population is in danger of 'genocide'. In this case, using the word aims at prompting the consciousness of public opinion and then leading the way to international intervention. Third, *legal issues* of course, when prosecuting the instigators and perpetrators, such as [former Chilean dictator Augusto] Pinochet or [former president of Serbia and Yugoslavia Slobodan] Milosevic for the crime of genocide or crimes against humanity.

Last but not least, the term can also be employed as a *weapon against one's enemy*. For example, the Serbs of Kosovo claimed to be the victims of a new genocide by the Albanians since the middle of the 1980s, while delegates at the Conference of Durban in 2001 accused Israel of perpetrating a 'real' genocide against the Palestinian people. As a result, the word is obviously employed as a symbolic shield in order to construct the identity of the victim—as a sword is drawn against an enemy.

Could we hope for some clarifications from the research community? Not really. The range of definitions is wide, from the psychologist Israel Charny who thinks that any massacre is genocide (including the nuclear accident at Chernobyl) to the historian Stephan Katz who supports the view that only one genocide was perpetrated in history, that against the Jews. However, some Jewish historians of the Holocaust are more open to comparison, such as Omer Bartov.

Origins of the Word "Genocide"

One of the most relevant reasons why genocide scholars are so divided is linked to the origins of the word 'genocide' itself. That is, at the point where international law and social science intersect. This can be seen clearly in Lemkin's chapter in his book of 1944 [*Axis Rule in Occupied Europe: Laws of Occupation Analysis of Government, Proposals for Redress*], in which he used the word 'genocide' for the first time. To sum up Lemkin's thought, he said: 'Here is a new phenomenon that is taking place in Europe. This new phenomenon requires a new term. I am coining the term "genocide"'. Then, he concluded his work by putting forward legal recommendations for struggling against this new crime form on an international level. Most genocide studies since Lemkin are precisely the outcome of that original conception.

The field of genocide studies was born out of the law. For proof of this, one need only survey the main pioneers' books in this field of research, for example [those] written by Leo Kuper, Helen Fein, Franck Chalk and Kurt Jonassohn. Almost all of them begin with a presentation and discussion of the United Nations convention of 1948. It is a known fact that the text of the convention contains deficiencies, even contradictions, which I shall not reconsider here. That has led to much debate and controversy among researchers. Opinions are divided over the place for the definition given by the United Nations, considering that this is a legal definition that is not so easy to handle in history or political sociology. For example, the 1948 [Genocide] Convention gives a central place to 'the intention to destroy a group as such' (Article 2). But applying this notion to history is problematic.

Some catastrophic events do not seem to have been 'desired' or willed, such as the famine of 1958–1962 in Communist China (where there were between 20 and 43 million deaths). Nobody can prove to date that Mao [Zedong, leader of Communist China,] in his delirious 'Great Leap Forward' intended to destroy his people. This hecatomb [multivictim sacrifice] is due more to the rigidity of the Communist Party, its voluntarist utopianism, its economic incompetence, and so on. On the other hand, in the case of the famine in Ukraine in 1932–1933 (which led to 6–7 millions deaths), the criminal will of [Soviet leader Joseph] Stalin is much more identifiable. There is no doubt that Moscow wanted to destroy any hotbed of resistance there definitively. Is this then a form of genocide? For some yes, for others not, since the destructive intention of Stalin did not aim to eliminate the Ukrainian people as such.

Other populations were decimated by hunger (Cossacks, Kouban, Central Asia . . .). Whatever these contradictory views, the trap that continuously threatens the historian is to become him/herself the prosecutor who will have to prove that all was calculated in advance. Of course history is made up of political will and strategic calculation, but also of a combination of circumstances, uncertainties; in short it is indeterminate.

Genocide Is Difficult to Understand

Mark Levene

Mark Levene is a noted genocide scholar and the director of the Parkes Institute for the Study of Jewish/Non-Jewish Relations at the University of Southampton in England. In the following excerpt from his book The Meaning of Genocide, *Levene contends that the definition of genocide found in the United Nations Convention on the Prevention and Punishment of Genocide does not adequately describe the true nature of the phenomenon because genocide is always contingent on unforeseen events. Levene identifies the concept of thc modern state as being the key actor that distinguishes mass murder from genocide, and purports that any attempt to understand genocide can only take place in the framework of historical development.*

How should we understand the term genocide? ... Why not ... begin with the official version, the 1984 United Nations Convention on the Prevention and Punishment of Genocide (thereafter UNC)? The Convention's key article—Article II—does clearly define genocide: as 'acts committed with intent to destroy in whole or in part, a national, ethnical, racial or religious group.' Many scholars in the field have found this definition flawed and unsatisfactory while others have deferred to it simply because in international law it is canonical. This author also disputes the value of the UNC as a tool for understanding the nature of genocide. Whether it has any value as a means for either preventing or punishing human rights violations is for others to decide.

Mark Levene, "Definitional Conundrums," from *The Meaning of Genocide*. London and New York: I.B. Tauris, 2005. Copyright © Mark Levene 2005. All rights reserved. Reproduced by permission.

Genocide Is Contingent on Events

However, my interest here in offering an alternative formulation is primarily to do with historical process. The UNC would appear to define genocide as something which has a pre-existing teleology [an ultimate purpose or design] almost to the point where the actors responsible for genocide were governed by a fixed and given blueprint of what they were going to do. It may be in many, if not the majority of such cases, that there exists—at least in the actors' heads, if not on paper—a prescript of this sort. But translating it into action is contingent on events, very often events which, far from being expected or foretold, actually, literally, came out of the blue. This is not to deny, then, that intention may not be a key factor in the act; it is simply to propose that the actuality of genocide, in practice, like all human-made catastrophes, is dependent on a form of collision between the avowed interests and intentions of the actors and the very complex, not to say capricious nature of contingency. . . .

It is worth studying the many instances of genocide, as a totality, for the very reason that they do have a not only remarkably common but also consistent set of causative ingredients. This does not mean that the study of genocide can be an exact science reducible to a mathematical equation. But it is, nevertheless, chartable as a phenomenon (albeit one that also repeatedly merges into others along a continuum of extreme violence) and, in so doing, links similar cases across time and space into a sinuous yet discernible pattern.

Genocide Requires Some Notion of "State"

Proper sense cannot be made of this pattern, however, without foregrounding the very actor—the modern state—notable by its remarkable absence in the UNC, even though again, . . . what exactly constitutes a state in cases of genocide might itself be open to further scrutiny. By the same token, while agreeing that the *genos* in genocide, as a term for representing the biological connectedness of those killed, is the most appropriate term available with regard to the phenomenon, our formulation would dispute that using a series of fixed labels—ethnical, racial or whatever—tells us very much about what turns state actors genocidal or who it is that is the object of their wrath. That said, our formulation is of a particular type of mass murder: one which is directed against 'some', not 'any', and involves direct physical killing of the targeted population. It also infers, though perhaps less explicitly spells out, that genocide has spatial and temporal characteristics that cannot be simply equated to a single episode of mass murder but, rather, point to a definite sequence of killing taking place in different, if usually geographically linked locations, though also at some juncture coming to a definite end. Above all, it is a formulation which seeks implicitly to suggest that this is a particular type of experience which has emerged out of a broader process of historical development and which has shaped not only how we understand ourselves as social organisms but also our place in the world.

Genocide Did Occur in Kosovo

Peter Ronayne

Peter Ronayne is a senior faculty member and international affairs coordinator at the Federal Executive Institute in Charlottesville, Virginia. In the following viewpoint he argues that genocide did in fact occur in Kosovo in 1999. In agreement with the Bill Clinton administration, Great Britain, NATO, and other world organizations, Ronayne asserts that the Serbs did commit genocide against the Kosovo Albanians, because their acts clearly fit the legal definition of genocide articulated by the 1948 UN Genocide Convention.

The American-led North Atlantic Treaty Organization (NATO) attack on Slobodan Milosevic's Yugoslavia beginning on 24 March 1999, represented the culmination of years of tension, hostility, and growing genocidal fervor in an already violence-wracked region. The Kosovo crisis and subsequent NATO air war against Yugoslavia teemed with issues central to the fields of genocide studies, world politics, and contemporary foreign policy. . . .

Diplomatic Intervention in the Kosovo Crisis

As a result of Balkan violence earlier in the decade, beginning in late 1997, the United Nations (UN), the North Atlantic Treaty Organization (NATO), the European Union (EU), the Organization for Security and Co-operation in Europe (OSCE) and the Contact Group, comprising France, Germany, Italy, Russia, Great Britain, and the United States, paid growing attention to the escalating ethnic tension in Kosovo. U.S. and

Peter Ronayne, "Genocide in Kosovo," *Human Rights Review*, vol. 5, issue 4, July–September 2004. Reproduced by permission.

European attention spiked in March 1998, following the killings by Serbian forces of some fifty-three Kosovo Albanians (half of whom were women and children) in response to a KLA [Kosovo Liberation Army, a guerrilla organization composed of ethnic Albanians] attack near Drenica.

Throughout 1998, the Contact Group promoted diplomatic efforts to find a peaceful, negotiated solution in Kosovo. Despite these international efforts, the violence grew and with it the emerging specter of another round of "ethnic cleansing" (basically a 1990s synonym for genocide) in the Balkans. At the end of March, the United Nations Security Council imposed sanctions, but a wary West still continued to hope that, as in the [1995] Dayton Accords, which ended the broader Balkan conflict, diplomacy would work without the need for significant use of force.

"Ethnic Cleansing" in Kosovo

But by mid September 1998, an estimated 250,000 Kosovo Albanians had been driven from their homes, and some 50,000 were still in the open as the winter approached. On 23 September, the UN Security Council adopted resolution 1199, which highlighted an impending human catastrophe in Kosovo, and demanded a ceasefire and the start of real political dialogue. The following day, NATO defense ministers meeting in Portugal affirmed their willingness and determination to take action if required. After twenty-one members of an Albanian family were massacred in Gorjne Obrinje, the West applied new pressure. On 13 October, U.S. envoy Richard Holbrooke reported that Slobodan Milosevic had agreed to the deployment of an unarmed OSCE verification mission to Kosovo to monitor, document, and publicly report violations. The agreement also allowed for a NATO aerial verification mission. The Federal Republic of Yugoslavia (FRY) authorities also agreed to reduce the numbers of security forces personnel in Kosovo. On 27 October, NATO agreed to keep compliance of the agreements, which were underpinned by UN Security Council resolution 1203, under continuous review and to remain prepared to carry out air strikes should they be required, given the continuing threat of a humanitarian crisis. Despite some doubts as to whether the Holbrooke agreements would deliver a lasting settlement, the international community recognized the opportunity they provided to allow those who had been forced from their homes to return, and was thus determined to try to make them work.

Nineteen-ninety-eight ended with relative calm. Despite the tempered hopes of those involved, a temporary stabilization of the situation, and the withdrawal of some Serb forces, the violence soon returned, as Serbs repositioned and the KLA maneuvered to take advantage of the OSCE-monitored cessation of hostilities. On 8 January 1999, KLA forces ambushed and killed three Serb policemen and killed another two days later. The Serbs responded harshly on 15 January at the village of Racak, killing forty-five ethnic Albanians, including a twelve-year-old boy and two women. Nine KLA soldiers were also killed. According to witnesses interviewed by Human Rights Watch (1999), "most of these men were fired upon from close range as they offered no resistance. The men's clothes were bloody, with slashes and holes at the same spots as their bullet entry and exit wounds, which argues against government claims that the victims were KLA soldiers who were dressed in civilian clothes after they had been killed. All of them were wearing rubber boots typical of Kosovo farmers rather than military footwear."

Racak was a significant turning point. Much like the Serb attack on the Sarajevo marketplace in August 1995, the Racak massacre galvanized Western outrage and energized NATO.

In response, NATO issued a "solemn warning" to Milosevic and the Kosovo Albanian leadership, reiterated the airstrikes threat, and moved additional military assets within range. On the diplomatic front, the FRY/Serbian and Kosovo Albanian leadership were summoned to talks at Rambouillet in France [in February 1999]. . . .

Genocide and Humanitarian War in Kosovo

As if on cue as talks collapsed, Yugoslav and irregular Serb forces launched a major offensive in Kosovo, accelerating their "ethnic cleansing" campaign and raising exponentially the fear of genocide. Through terror and violence, Serb forces drove the majority of Kosovo Albanians—some 1.5 million people—from their homes. Hundreds of settlements were burned and looted. Massacres led to innumerable mass graves in Kosovo and in Serbia proper. Mosques, religious sites, and schools were systematically destroyed. Rape re-emerged in the Balkans as a tool of organized, deliberate terror. At least 6,000 and as many as 11,000 Kosovar Albanians were murdered, with bodies burned in over 500 mass graves. This was not improvised violence or a mob reaction. A covert Serbian plan, code-named Operation Horseshoe, to expel Kosovo Albanians from their homeland had been drawn up months before and showed that while Milosevic was engaged in political theatre at Rambouillet, his forces had been preparing to destroy the Kosovar Albanians. Thus, whether officially "genocide" or not under the dictates of the United Nations Genocide Convention on the Prevention and Punishment of Genocide (UNCG), Serb actions in Kosovo were fully intentional, planned, and systematic.

The West Invokes the "G-Word"

In a prime time speech to the nation on 24 March, U.S. President Bill Clinton explained the resort to force and appealed to both "moral imperative" and national interests. Said Clinton, "America has a responsibility to stand with our allies when they are trying to save innocent lives and preserve peace, freedom, and stability in Europe. That is what we are doing in Kosovo." As the pace and scale of Serb violence increased,

German defense minister Rudolf Scharping, on 28 March, deployed the "g-word," stating in a television interview that "information reaching us indicates that a genocide has begun. We must prevent that from happening." The next day, U.S. State Department officials remarked that "genocide is unfolding" in Kosovo and that NATO strikes would end only when Milosevic accepted the U.S.-brokered peace plan. From the U.S. legislative branch, Senate majority leader Bob Dole urged NATO to stay the course and expand targeting in the effort to "end genocide in the Balkans once and for all."

Britain's leadership joined the chorus with British defense secretary George Robertson saying, "We are confronting a regime which is intent on genocide." Added NATO spokesman Jamie Shea, "Whether we like it or not, we have to admit that we are on the brink of a major humanitarian disaster in Kosovo, the likes of which have not been seen in Europe since the closing stages of World War II."

Solving Kosovo's humanitarian disaster proved more difficult and lengthy than initially suspected. Armed with a set of faulty assumptions from the Dayton experience (namely that Milosevic would quickly cave in to any sustained show of NATO force), optimistic observers anticipated an air campaign of as little as three days. Instead, it took Operation Allied Force almost three months to compel Serb capitulation.

On 10 June, following seventy-eight days of bombing, agreement was finalized under which Serb forces would withdraw and Kosovo would remain part of Serbia but under UN/NATO protection and with significant international oversight and monitoring. Nearly all of the displaced Kosovar Albanians returned to the province following the war. Kosovo has been governed by the UN Interim Administration Mission in Kosovo (UNMIK) since June 1999, under the authority of UN Security Council Resolution 1244.

Future Challenges

The crisis in Kosovo raised rather than solved a host of pressing challenges for the field of genocide studies and world politics in general. Perhaps the most fundamental and rather complex question at stake is the future legitimacy and legality of such humanitarian interventions, particularly given the limits of a fractured UN system that finds itself schizophrenically torn between the mandates of state sovereignty and noninterference and the rising concern over protection of individual sovereignty and human rights. Serious concerns remain about the UN, specifically about the Security Council's future ability to navigate these clashing norms in world politics. . . .

As of this writing (February 2004), Milosevic stands trial for charges filed in three indictments related to crimes committed in Kosovo, Croatia, and Bosnia.[1] However, only the Bosnia indictment includes the specific charge of genocide. For his role and responsibility for actions in Kosovo in 1999, Milosevic faces charges for crimes against humanity and violations of the customs of war. The genocide charge is curiously absent despite the fact that the arc of crime and atrocity in Kosovo seems to fit the Convention's legal definition quite neatly, including: (1) killing members of a national, ethnic, racial or religious group; (2) causing serious bodily or mental harm to members of the group; and (3) deliberately inflicting on the group conditions of life calculated to bring about its physical destruction in whole or in part. Consistent application of the UN Genocide Convention in the pursuit of justice, especially given the emerging International Criminal Court (ICC), is of utmost importance, and the Kosovo issue is a critical case in this unfolding process.

1. Milosevic died of a heart attack on March 11, 2006, in his cell at The Hague detention center. With only 50 hours left of testimony remaining before the close of his trial, some have speculated that his heart attack might have been brought on deliberately despite Milosevic's poor health from high blood pressure and diabetes. In June 2006, the Supreme Court of Serbia convicted Milosevic of ordering the murders of political opponents Iran Stambolic and VUK Draskovic.

Genocide Did Not Occur in Kosovo

Martin Mennecke

In the following viewpoint Martin Mennecke, doctoral student in international law in the Department of Holocaust and Genocide Studies at the Danish Institute for International Studies, argues that the events that occurred in Kosovo in the 1990s do not constitute genocide. Given that there is no evidence that the Serbs intended to target ethnic Albanians for slaughter, these acts should be classified as crimes against humanity instead. In fact, Mennecke notes, the Serbs helped move some of the Kosovo Albanians to safety.

Before the Yugoslav wars began in Slovenia in 1991, the autonomous province of Kosovo had been viewed as the most likely location for an outburst of ethnic violence. In contrast to the other Yugoslav republics, where the various ethnic groups had—with the important exception of World War II—lived together in relative peace, Kosovo had for a long time been the site of ethnic tensions, particularly following (and not long after) [former leader Josip Broz, aka Marshal] Tito's death in 1981. It was also Kosovo, in the late 1990s, that brought the international spotlight back to former Yugoslavia, as it became the site of frequent discrimination and isolated acts of violence against the Albanians. Eventually these hostilities were replaced by full-scale ethnic cleansing, which ultimately prompted an armed intervention by NATO [North American Treaty Organization] starting in March 1999. Then, as now, the issue relevant to legal bodies such as the International Criminal Tribunal for the Former Yugoslavia (ICTY), but also to politicians and scholars, is whether the events of Kosovo justified the label "genocide."

Background to the Conflict

A key factor in the dispute between Serbs and Albanians was that Kosovo played a special role in Serbian ideology because of a battle in 1389 and the legendary significance attributed to it in the public memory. At the same time, Kosovo was predominately populated by Albanians (approximately 90 percent of the population) and steered by an Albanian-dominated regional government. The series of harsh, anti-Albanian measures introduced in the late 1980s and early 1990s by the new Yugoslav leader Slobodan Milosevic were a response to the perceived marginalization of Kosovo-Serbs and increased the political tensions in Kosovo considerably.

The international community, however, chose to refrain from interfering in this explosive situation. The decision not to present an outline for the future of Kosovo at the Bosnian peace talks in Dayton, Ohio, in November 1995 proved to be a detrimental omission, as it weakened the position of moderate leaders such as Ibrahim Rugova and radicalized the Albanians. Soon after, by 1997, an armed separatist movement, the so-called Kosovo Liberation Army (KLA), began to commit attacks primarily on Serb police forces, but also on Kosovar "collaborators."

The Serb response towards the Kosovar opposition and isolated acts of terror by the KLA was frequently indiscriminate and disproportionate, even if officially aimed exclusively at KLA fighters and their strongholds. In a campaign that resembled the war in Bosnia, Serb forces attacked villages, killed and brutalized inhabitants, and burned down houses in order to force them to leave. By the end of 1998, approximately 3,000 Kosovo Albanians had been killed and more than 300,000 expelled from their homes. In 1999, the Serb campaign to create a Serb majority in Kosovo by means of ethnic cleansing continued, only temporarily put on hold when international negotiations or the presence of international observers required it.

In the course of the conflict, approximately 800,000 of the roughly 2 million Kosovo Albanians fled the province to neighboring countries, while several hundred thousands more became internally displaced persons. The number of Albanians killed continues to be unclear. Nongovernmental organizations' (NGOs') estimates range between 5000 and 30,000 victims, while Milosevic has been charged with responsibility for the murder of more than 900 Kosovo Albanians. The figure of more than 100,000 victims, which was indirectly suggested by NATO officials and Western politicians in the context of justifying the military intervention that started in March 1999, seems to be greatly exaggerated.

The Response of the International Community

The international community seriously turned to the Kosovo issue only in the fall of 1998. In October of that year, the Serbs and Albanians agreed to a verification mission of the Organization for Security and Cooperation in Europe (OSCE) in order to establish an enduring truce. Sent originally as an impartial, mutually accepted observer, the OSCE mission soon was perceived by the Serbs as biased towards the Albanians since the KLA was not hindered from taking advantage of the international presence when it renewed its military activities.

It was in this context that the OSCE brought the "massacre of Racak"—in which Serb forces had allegedly cold-bloodedly executed 45 villagers on January 15, 1999—to the attention of the international media. Despite Serb efforts to explain the deaths as resulting from battles between KLA and police units, this news became a turning point in the hitherto reluctant public debate on armed humanitarian intervention in Kosovo. Even with the international pressure growing, however, the Serb government refused to sign an agreement brokered by the multinational Contact Group at Rambouillet, France, in February and March 1999. The Serbs mainly did so because the agreement envisaged a strong NATO force to supervise its implementation and opened the possibility for a future referendum on Kosovo's independence (see the agreement at www.unmikonline.org/scdocs.htm).

Western politicians subsequently overcame their inhibitions against applying military means because they feared that they yet again were, as in Bosnia, manipulated by the Milosevic regime. On March 24, 1999, NATO launched, without the prerequisite mandate of the United Nations Security Council, a 78-day-long bombing campaign against Serbia and its troops deployed in Kosovo. Given the use of controversial weaponry such as cluster bombs and the considerable damage reportedly caused to civilians and civilian targets, the NATO air campaign raised serious concerns about possible violations of international humanitarian law.

In Kosovo itself, the NATO airstrikes initially only reinforced and speeded up Serbian attempts to expel Kosovo Albanians from the region. The intervening Western governments had hoped that, after a few days of bombing, Milosevic would return to the negotiation table, but they misjudged how the Serbs would react to the NATO air campaign. At the same time, NATO governments could not mount the political will to send in ground troops, as they wanted to minimize the risk of their own casualties.

Only in the end did NATO succeed in forcing Belgrade [Serbia's capital] to withdraw its forces from the province and secure the return of Albanians who had been expelled from their homes. A tragic, and insufficiently known, side effect of this return of the Albanians is that the local Kosovo Serb population became itself victim of acts of revenge and ethnic cleansing; more than 100,000 Serbs fled Kosovo after the armed fighting ended in June 1999, and several hundred Serbs were killed. Today [2004], some 47,000 international Kosovo Protection Force troops, over 4,000 international police officers, and 16,000 UN administrative staff continue to keep the fragile peace and to secure the rebuilding of the ethnically riven province.

The Question of Genocide

Numerous human rights NGOs, such as Physicians for Human Rights (1999) and the International Helsinki Federation (1999), have argued that the Kosovo Albanians became victims of genocide. Others, such as Human Rights Watch and Amnesty International, harshly criticized the Serb conduct and called on the ICTY to investigate possible war crimes, but stopped short of labeling it genocide. A similar, equally undecided debate ensued among political decision-makers; in the U.S. government and U.S. Congress, supporters of a NATO intervention tended to invoke the genocide label while others rejected this classification and explicit attempts to draw parallels to the Holocaust. On the legal front, it is significant to note that the ICTY has not indicted anybody for the crime of genocide in regard to the events in Kosovo. Milosevic, for example, [stood] trial for his alleged responsibility for the ethnic cleansing of Kosovo, but [was] indicted only for war crimes and crimes against humanity. Another semi-international court, the UN-supervised Supreme Court of Kosovo, confirmed that there had been "a systematic campaign of terror including murders, rapes, arsons and severe maltreatments" of Albanians, but also found that "the exactions committed by Milosevic's regime cannot be qualified as criminal acts of genocide, since their purpose was not the destruction of the Albanian ethnic group—but its forceful departure from Kosovo."

In terms of the legal definition of genocide, the crucial element is the intent of the perpetrator to destroy in whole or in part a particular group, as such. The fact that hundreds of thousands of Kosovo Albanians were deported by the Serbs via trains and trucks to the border to Albania or Macedonia speaks against an intent to destroy the group. In addition, no reports have yet established that the Serb paramilitary forces singled out—as they had done in Bosnia—community leaders or "battle-aged" men for execution—a pattern that could have suggested genocidal intent. Instead, this campaign of ethnic cleansing, including widespread murders, could legally be classified as crimes against humanity.

Conclusion

Such a conclusion—genocide was not committed in Kosovo—stands in stark contrast to how frequently decision-makers used the stigmatizing term "genocide" when referring to Kosovo. The German Defence Secretary Rudolf Scharping (1999), for example, stated that "[t]he genocide has begun" (quoted in Associated Press, March 29, n.p.), and his British counterpart George Robertson declared that "[t]hese airstrikes have one purpose only: to stop the genocidal violence."

Does the end—the humanitarian intervention on behalf of the victims—justify the inaccurate use of means (e.g., the use of the label "genocide")? Labeling the conduct of the Serb forces in Kosovo genocidal undoubtedly smoothed the way for armed intervention without the requisite UN Security Council mandate and thus emphasized the potential of the term "genocide"—not least in light of the fruitless discussions at the United Nations in 1994, in the wake of the Rwanda genocide. After all, the aerial attacks on Serbia were carried out without a mandate of the UN Security Council and thus constituted *prima facie* [sufficient evidence] a violation of the prime rule of international law—that is, of the prohibition of the use of force. At the same time, other massive human rights violations, such as crimes against humanity, deserve similar concern and can demand armed intervention; but deeming them all genocide is neither wise nor accurate. Indeed, the political utilization of the heavily connotated term "genocide" in relation to the Kosovo conflict reinforces ongoing concerns about the abuse and trivialization of the term.

Genocide Is Occurring in Darfur

Andrew B. Loewenstein

Andrew B. Loewenstein, a Boston-based international lawyer who served on the Atrocities Documentation Team commissioned by the U.S. State Department to interview Darfur refugees in eastern Chad, states in the following viewpoint that there is no question that genocide is occurring in Darfur, Sudan, in Africa. Loewenstein demonstrates through survivor interviews and other testimony that the Sudanese government is intent on eliminating targeted ethnic groups, which is a key qualification for labeling mass killings genocide.

A 30-year-old woman squats on the sand outside her tent in eastern Chad's Touloum refugee camp as she tells me about her escape from Darfur. Her family, members of the Zaghawa ethnic group, had been farmers near the town of Kutum in Northern Darfur. She describes how, before fleeing to this desolate place, Sudanese soldiers and Janjaweed [Arabic Muslim] militias killed her husband and son, then burned her village. She recounts how she fled with other survivors, and how, during her escape, she became separated from three young boys with whom she was traveling. When she found them again, their throats had been cut, their hands chopped off, and their feet sliced from the big toe to the ankle. She saw that their heads had been broken open and their brains removed. Also, their penises had been cut off.

Killings Deemed Not Genocide

In the summer of 2004, I served on a team of lawyers and other investigators commissioned by the [U.S.] State Department to travel to Chad to interview survivors of the massacres

Andrew B. Loewenstein, "Words Fail," *New Republic*, vol. 234, issue 18, May 15, 2006. Copyright © 2006 by The New Republic, Inc. Reproduced by permission of *The New Republic*.

in Darfur. Shortly after we returned—and based on our interviews—[U.S. former secretary of state] Colin Powell made his now-famous declaration that "genocide has been committed in Darfur." But, since then, other key international organizations—Amnesty International, Human Rights Watch, and, most importantly, the United Nations—have declined to characterize the atrocities in Darfur as genocide. The U.N.'s decision was particularly significant. Unlike other groups, which merely failed to weigh in on the question, the United Nations affirmatively declared that the Sudanese government had not committed genocide. It's not clear what prompted the United Nations to make this excessively cautious pronouncement. It certainly wasn't for lack of evidence.

On September 18, 2004, the [UN] Security Council passed Resolution 1564, which directed [UN secretary general] Kofi Annan to establish a Commission of Inquiry on Darfur to determine whether genocide had taken place. To be found culpable for genocide, one must commit certain criminal acts, such as killing or causing serious bodily or mental harm; and—this is the key part—these acts must be committed with the specific intent to destroy, in whole or in part, a national, ethnic, racial, or religious group. When the Commission reported back several months later, it acknowledged that the government and Janjaweed had committed acts enumerated in the 1948 Genocide Convention and thus were likely culpable for war crimes and crimes against humanity. But it also absolved Khartoum [Sudan's capital] of genocide charges. "[T]he crucial element of genocidal intent appears to be missing, at least as far as the central Government authorities are concerned," the group wrote.

Conferring Genocidal Intent

Yet the stories survivors told me made clear that Sudan intended to eliminate the targeted groups. One man recounted witnessing Janjaweed leader Musa Hilal announce in a village marketplace that the Sudanese government had sent him to "kill all the blacks in this area"—a reference to the region's non-Arab tribes. Hilal, this man recalled, declared that his forces would "give the Arab people freedom" by "clear[ing] the land until the desert"—that is, the populated areas of Darfur. Another refugee, who lived near a Janjaweed training camp, explained that she heard the militia being ordered over a loudspeaker to "kill" the "Zaghawa people" of the nine surrounding villages. Still another told how she and six other women were captured by 30 Janjaweed who raped and beat them with leather whips. The Janjaweed's intentions were unmistakable, she said: They shouted, invoking a local racial slur, "We must kill the Nuba."

Even putting aside the perpetrators' statements, the Commission could have inferred genocidal intent by drawing upon the extensive jurisprudence on genocide generated by the war-crimes trials for the former Yugoslavia and Rwanda. The U.N. Yugoslavia tribunal judged Bosnian-Serb commander Radislav Krstíic to have had genocidal intent based, in part, on evidence that his forces killed Bosnian males old enough to bear arms without regard to whether they actually served in the military. That precedent surely applies to Darfur, where young children, particularly boys—and even the unborn—are specifically targeted. Consider a mother who told me that soldiers inspected her seven-day-old infant to determine its sex. Upon discovering it was a boy, one soldier declared the male child had to be killed (but, in a moment of conscience, another soldier prevailed upon him to spare the boy's life). The soldiers' explanation for contemplating infanticide? "We are sent by Omar Al Bashir"—Sudan's president—"to kill you because you are black." Or consider a woman who reported witnessing 15 boys—ranging in age from four to 15—rounded up and summarily executed. Or the many boys thrown into burning huts. Or the pregnant woman whose attackers stripped her clothes and then, using a boot, beat her abdomen to kill her fetus, because, they said, the unborn baby would be the "son of a black man." These are not the hallmarks of counterinsurgency warfare, as the Commission described Sudan's campaign, but of something much more sinister: a calculated program to eliminate entire ethnic groups.

The Sudanese Government's Role

There should be no doubt that Sudan's central government was behind this. The man who told of witnessing Hilal's marketplace speech recounted how the Janjaweed leader was accompanied by a uniformed military officer, who instructed the crowd to obey Hilal's commands. Hilal himself has acknowledged he acted on behalf of the governing regime. Ground assaults on villages were invariably preceded by bombardment from the Sudanese air force's fleet of Antonov bombers, MiGs, and helicopter gunships; and survivors almost universally reported to me that their attackers included contingents from both the Janjaweed, who rode horses and camels, and the Sudanese military, who arrived in vehicles. As Human Rights Watch has noted, the Khartoum regime and the Janjaweed work "hand-in-glove."

Even if the Commission felt it didn't have sufficient evidence of genocidal intent in the capital, it should have stated that it couldn't yet make a determination because of the government's obstruction. The regime certainly provided ample justification for such a finding: For instance, First Vice President Ali Osman Mohammed Taha and Defense Minister Bakri Hassan Salih promised the Commission key documents that never materialized.

The commission's failure to call genocide by its name is not just an academic quibble over legal nomenclature. By absolving Sudan of this crime, it released the international community from its responsibility under the Genocide Convention to "prevent" this "odious scourge." Moreover, Sudan, which received an advance copy of the report, seized the opportunity to trumpet the no-genocide finding to the press. Subsequent headlines represented an enormous propaganda victory for the regime: "UN rules out genocide in Darfur" (BBC); "UN Report: Darfur not genocide" (CNN); "Sudan Killings in Darfur Not Genocide, Says UN Report" (*The Financial Times*); and so on.

I interviewed only one Zaghawa man who had been captured and yet survived. He explained how his camouflage-wearing captors had wanted to kill him and how, when objections were raised, they took him to their leader, who decided to spare his life—an act that, in the leader's words, contradicted his "orders" from the "Sudanese government." In Darfur, this man's exception proves the genocidal rule.

Genocide Is Not Occurring in Darfur

United Nations International Commission

In 2004, the United Nations requested a commission be formed to investigate escalating violence in Darfur, Sudan. In the following viewpoint the commission argues that while the acts occurring in Darfur are crimes against humanity and war crimes, they do not constitute genocide as it is defined by the Convention on Genocide. According to the commission, the absence of genocidal intent is the crucial missing element in making this declaration.

Acting under Chapter VII of the United Nations Charter, on 18 September 2004 the Security Council adopted resolution 1564 requesting, *inter alia* [among other things], that the Secretary-General 'rapidly establish an international commission of inquiry in order immediately to investigate reports of violations of international humanitarian law and human rights law in Darfur by all parties, to determine also whether or not acts of genocide have occurred, and to identify the perpetrators of such violations with a view to ensuring that those responsible are held accountable'. . . .

The Commission assembled in Geneva [Switzerland] and began its work on 25 October 2004.

In order to discharge its mandate, the Commission endeavoured to fulfil four key tasks: (1) to investigate reports of violations of international humanitarian law and human rights law in Darfur by all parties; (2) to determine whether or not acts of genocide have occurred; (3) to identify the perpetrators of violations of international humanitarian law and hu-

United Nations International Commission, "Report of the International Commission of Inquiry on Darfur Report to the Secretary-General," January 2005. www.un.org/News/ dh/sudan/com_inq_darfur.pdf. Reprinted with the permission of the United Nations.

man rights law in Darfur; and (4) to suggest means of ensuring that those responsible for such violations are held accountable. While the Commission considered all events relevant to the current conflict in Darfur, it focused in particular on incidents that occurred between February 2003 and mid-January 2005. . . .

Violations of Human Rights Law

The Commission took as the starting point for its work two irrefutable facts regarding the situation in Darfur. Firstly, according to United Nations estimates there are 1.65 million internally displaced persons in Darfur, and more than 200,000 refugees from Darfur in neighbouring Chad. Secondly, there has been large-scale destruction of villages throughout the three states of Darfur. The Commission conducted independent investigations to establish additional facts and gathered extensive information on multiple incidents of violations affecting villages, towns and other locations across North, South and West Darfur. The conclusions of the Commission are based on the evaluation of the facts gathered or verified through its investigations.

Based on a thorough analysis of the information gathered in the course of its investigations, the Commission established that the Government of the Sudan and the Janjaweed are responsible for serious violations of international human rights and humanitarian law amounting to crimes under international law. In particular, the Commission found that Government forces and militias conducted indiscriminate attacks, including killing of civilians, torture, enforced disappearances, destruction of villages, rape and other forms of sexual violence, pillaging and forced displacement, throughout Darfur. These acts were conducted on a widespread and systematic basis, and therefore may amount to crimes against humanity. The extensive destruction and displacement have resulted in a loss of livelihood and means of survival for countless women,

men and children. In addition to the large scale attacks, many people have been arrested and detained, and many have been held *incommunicado* for prolonged periods and tortured. The vast majority of the victims of all of these violations have been from the Fur, Zaghawa, Massalit, Jebel, Aranga and other so-called 'African' tribes.

In their discussions with the Commission, Government of the Sudan officials stated that any attacks carried out by Government armed forces in Darfur were for counter-insurgency purposes and were conducted on the basis of military imperatives. However, it is clear from the Commission's findings that most attacks were deliberately and indiscriminately directed against civilians. Moreover even if rebels, or persons supporting rebels, were present in some of the villages—which the Commission considers likely in only a very small number of instances—the attackers did not take precautions to enable civilians to leave the villages or otherwise be shielded from attack. Even where rebels may have been present in villages, the impact of the attacks on civilians shows that the use of military force was manifestly disproportionate to any threat posed by the rebels.

The Commission is particularly alarmed that attacks on villages, killing of civilians, rape, pillaging and forced displacement have continued during the course of the Commission's mandate. The Commission considers that action must be taken urgently to end these violations.

While the Commission did not find a systematic or a widespread pattern to these violations, it found credible evidence that rebel forces, namely members of the SLA [Sudan Liberation Army] and JEM [Justice and Equality Movement], also are responsible for serious violations of international human rights and humanitarian law which may amount to war crimes. In particular, these violations include cases of murder of civilians and pillage.

Have Acts of Genocide Occurred?

The Commission concluded that the Government of the Sudan has not pursued a policy of genocide. Arguably, two elements of genocide might be deduced from the gross violations of human rights perpetrated by Government forces and the militias under their control. These two elements are, first, the *actus reus* [guilt-proving evidence] consisting of killing, or causing serious bodily or mental harm, or deliberately inflicting conditions of life likely to bring about physical destruction; and, second, on the basis of a subjective standard, the existence of a protected group being targeted by the authors of criminal conduct. However, the crucial element of genocidal intent appears to be missing, at least as far as the central Government authorities are concerned. Generally speaking the policy of attacking, killing and forcibly displacing members of some tribes does not evince a specific intent to annihilate, in whole or in part, a group distinguished on racial, ethnic, national or religious grounds. Rather, it would seem that those who planned and organized attacks on villages pursued the intent to drive the victims from their homes, primarily for purposes of counter-insurgency warfare.

The Commission does recognise that in some instances individuals, including Government officials, may commit acts with genocidal intent. Whether this was the case in Darfur, however, is a determination that only a competent court can make on a case by case basis.

The conclusion that no genocidal policy has been pursued and implemented in Darfur by the Government authorities, directly or through the militias under their control, should not be taken in any way as detracting from the gravity of the crimes perpetrated in that region. International offences such as the crimes against humanity and war crimes that have been committed in Darfur may be no less serious and heinous than genocide.

Identification of Perpetrators

The Commission has collected reliable and consistent elements which indicate the responsibility of some individuals for serious violations of international human rights law and international humanitarian law, including crimes against humanity or war crimes, in Darfur. In order to identify perpetrators, the Commission decided that there must be 'a reliable body of material consistent with other verified circumstances, which tends to show that a person may reasonably be suspected of being involved in the commission of a crime.' The Commission therefore makes an assessment of likely suspects, rather than a final judgment as to criminal guilt.

Those identified as possibly responsible for the above-mentioned violations consist of individual perpetrators, including officials of the Government of Sudan, members of militia forces, members of rebel groups, and certain foreign army officers acting in their personal capacity. Some Government officials, as well as members of militia forces, have also been named as possibly responsible for joint criminal enterprise to commit international crimes. Others are identified for their possible involvement in planning and/or ordering the commission of international crimes, or of aiding and abetting the perpetration of such crimes. The Commission also has identified a number of senior Government officials and military commanders who may be responsible, under the notion of superior (or command) responsibility, for knowingly failing to prevent or repress the perpetration of crimes. Members of rebel groups are named as suspected of participating in a joint criminal enterprise to commit international crimes, and as possibly responsible for knowingly failing to prevent or repress the perpetration of crimes committed by rebels. . . .

Accountability Mechanisms

The Commission strongly recommends that the Security Council immediately refer the situation of Darfur to the International Criminal Court [ICC], pursuant to article 13(b) of the ICC Statute. As repeatedly stated by the Security Council, the situation constitutes a threat to international peace and security. Moreover, as the Commission has confirmed, serious violations of international human rights law and humanitarian law by all parties are continuing. The prosecution by the ICC of persons allegedly responsible for the most serious crimes in Darfur would contribute to the restoration of peace in the region.

CHAPTER 2

The Origins of Genocide

Professionals Legitimize Acts of Genocide

Alex Alvarez

Alex Alvarez is a criminal-justice professor at Northern Arizona University and the author of Governments, Citizens, and Genocide. *In the following viewpoint, taken from a paper given at an international genocide symposium, he argues that professionals, such as doctors, lawyers, and scientists, greatly contribute to the legitimization of genocide. They do so, he says, by creating and maintaining social environments that further stigmatize the peoples under attack. Because they are considered authority figures, professionals can easily manipulate others into accepting their ideologies. Regrettably, Alvarez notes, professionals are often co-opted by the leaders of genocidal campaigns based on the very nature of the professionals' work.*

I would like to spend a few minutes talking with you about the role that social elites play in legitimating genocide. It is by now well recognized that genocide requires the active participation of many members of a society and the passive acquiescence of many more. It is a crime of the many, rather than of the few. The Holocaust, for example, has been called a "German national project" because it involved so many participants and accomplices from all walks of life. Similarly, the Rwandan genocide, while guided and orchestrated by military and political leaders, nonetheless relied upon many ordinary citizens to facilitate the killing. Other examples of genocide also exhibit the same kind of mass participation and/or acceptance.

Since all genocides are large-scale and systematic attempts to eradicate populations, their perpetration is utterly depen-

Alex Alvarez, "Justifying Genocide: The Role of Professionals in Legitimitizing Mass Killing," *IDEA: A Journal of Social Issues*, December 20, 2001, from the History and Prevention of Genocide Symposium, Vienna, November 8–9, 2001. Reproduced by permission.

dent upon large segments of a nation going along with the genocidal policies. This raises the important question of why does this acceptance take place? How is it possible for genocidally inclined states to enlist such mass support in their destructive and murderous policies? Many of the individuals who participate are typically ordinary citizens who may well have values antithetical to violence and criminality. Although it is popular to view them as such, the perpetrators of genocide are not monsters or psychopaths. Most are ordinary human beings engaged in extraordinary crimes. The psychopaths and sadists are far outnumbered by individuals who are "normal" in their psychological processes. How is it possible for all of these participants to put aside their values and engage in genocide? While there is no single answer to these questions, and while a complete understanding of how these crimes occur must draw from a number of different disciplines and perspectives, I believe one important factor concerns the role that social elites play in providing important justifications for the violence.

Invariably, genocide receives much of its perceived legitimacy from professionals who provide the ideological, intellectual, scientific, and legal underpinnings for the destruction of a specific group. Because of their status and visibility certain professions are very important in legitimating the destructive actions of their states. Lawyers, doctors, and scientists often justify genocide by providing "vocabularies of motive" that frame the genocidal actions in such a way as to make it acceptable and palatable for the mass of a society. In all fairness, I should note that this complicity is not always intentional.

Sociologists have long recognized that most people have an innate willingness to defer to authority. Authority, it should be noted, is distinct from power. Power concerns the ability to achieve certain goals in spite of resistance and opposition. Authority, on the other hand, is the power that individuals and groups accept as legitimate. It is the difference between willingness and coercion. Most individuals voluntarily accept the demands and constraints of social living, deferring many of their own desires and needs in favor of those of the group. We are, after all, social beings, who are taught to get along and obey and to be respectful of "authority figures." This natural inclination to fit in with collectives is termed conformity and conformity is a powerful force for most individuals. . . .

All of us tend toward obedience and conformity, especially if someone in authority legitimates or authorizes the behavior or attitude. But how does this social reality translate into genocidal complicity?

The Role of Doctors and Scientists

First, genocidally inclined states often refer to a variety of scientific or pseudo-scientific ideas that can be utilized to justify later atrocities. Because they are "scientific" they have a weight and power that would otherwise be lacking. These ideas are disseminated by scientists and doctors whose status lends weight and importance to their pronouncements. While the original intent may have been completely unpolitical the ideas are perverted to suit a particular agenda. For example, in the years preceding the Nazi rise to power, medical professionals created a body of knowledge that was used to lethal effect against the Jews. The Nazis appropriated medical language and imagery to scapegoat the Jews for much of Germany's problems.

Around the beginning of the 20th century physicians throughout western Europe and North America became interested, even obsessed, with disease and its transmission. Diseases such as typhus, plague, cholera, smallpox, and influenza had long ravaged large segments of the world populations and during the latter half of the 19th century, Europe's colonial empire had brought a host of new infectious afflictions to European consciousness. Western doctors responded with a concerted campaign to make Europe and America safe by using sanitation and hygiene as preventative measures to combat these lethal outbreaks. Unfortunately they also began identifying Jews as carriers of disease, and in fact as disease themselves. Typhus, for example, became known as a Jewish disease or *Judenfieber* [Jewish fever]. It is no accident that the language of sanitation, hygiene, delousing, gas, and crematoria, first introduced to combat disease, became such notable features of the Holocaust.

Under the Nazis, these associations created the ideal situation for a self-fulfilling prophecy. The Jews could be segregated from the general population and concentrated into ghettos in order to prevent them from transmitting disease. Once they were crowded into ghettos and deprived of enough food and facilities for proper sanitation, the outbreak of disease in these places was inevitable but was attributed to the Jewish propensity to carry disease, not the conditions in the ghetto. In short, the Nazis were able to portray their discriminatory and genocidal actions as necessary to maintain the health and welfare of German society.

Doctors also played an active role in creating the mechanisms necessary for genocide to take place.... Many of the specific techniques for killing were pioneered by doctors during the infamous T4 euthanasia program [the Nazi policy of killing incurably ill, disabled and elderly people].

The Role of Nationalism

In a similar vein, the *Memorandum of the Serbian Academy of Sciences and Arts* set the stage for a resurgent Serb nationalism years before the ethnic cleansing and genocide actually took place. Published in 1986, the memorandum was a document that detailed a long list of injustices suffered by the Serb peoples. Since the 1970s, Serb intellectuals and academics had increasingly begun expressing increasingly nationalistic sentiments. Members of the Serbian academy of sciences and arts had begun meeting in 1983 to discuss the situation in Yugoslavia, which resulted in the memorandum of 1986.

In this memorandum the authors asserted that "in less than fifty years, within two consecutive generations, twice exposed to physical annihilation, forceful assimilation, religious conversion, cultural genocide, ideological indoctrination, invalidation, and denunciation of their own tradition under the imposed complex of guilt, intellectually and politically disarmed, the Serbian people were exposed to temptations that were too great not to leave deep scars on their spirit." Additionally, the memorandum asserted that "the Serbian people have a historic and democratic right to establish fully national and cultural integrity independently, regardless of the republic or province in which they live."

Essentially, this document provided a legitimation for the policies of "ethnic cleansing" which were to follow. The perpetrators were not perpetrating evil from this perspective, they were merely defending their people and asserting their rights. As the polarizing forces of the cold war faded away in the early 1990s, nationalism became the means by which unscrupulous politicians such as [former Serbian president] Slobodan Milosovic and [former Croatian president] Franjo Tudjman were able to remain in power.

The Role of Legal Professionals

Another important group that often plays a significant role in legitimating the persecution of various groups are legal professionals. Lawyers and judges throughout Germany, for example, did much to provide the legal foundation for the subsequent Holocaust. Not only does the profession of law carry with it a tremendous amount of prestige and status, but the law itself is a powerful vehicle in legitimating policies of persecution. By definition, everything that is legal is legitimate and everything that is illegal is illegitimate. The Holocaust happened only after legal initiatives had over the years deprived Jews of their professions, their possessions, and their rights. Once their rights were removed, anything could and did happen to them. Similarly, in Bosnia legal officials in the *Republika Srpska* [Serb Republic] enacted laws depriving Bosnian Muslims of their rights and legal protections.

In some communities, non-Serbs were barred from all management and senior positions in large businesses. In one town, non-Serbs had a curfew of 4:00 p.m., and were banned from gathering in public places, making contact with relatives who didn't live in the town, drive or travel by car, sell real estate without going through Serb authorities, or to leave without permission. In this legalistic way, the Muslim population was pressured into leaving Serb-controlled territory. These legal decrees had the effect of socially and economically marginalizing the non-Serb population, making them more vulnerable to more extreme measures.

Control of the law lends itself to ideological power. Simply put, the law is a tool of propaganda, lending credibility to certain groups, actions, and behaviors, and delegitimizing others. The ability to legally define certain people as criminal is to take away not only their rights, but also their identity as citizens. Criminals are generally perceived as different and alien from the "law abiding" and "decent" citizens of a society. The perpetrators of genocide, protected as they are by the state and its laws, are defined as good citizens engaged in a patriotic service to their nation. The victims of genocide, on the other hand, are portrayed as devious and scheming enemies who pose a threat to those being asked to kill them.

In this Orwellian universe, roles are reversed and victims are portrayed as perpetrators while the perpetrators see themselves as victims. In other words, the killers are provided with ideologies that alter perceptions of reality in order to justify their lethal behavior. As my colleague [criminologist] Jeff Ferrell reminds us, "authority operates not only through prison cells and poverty, but by constructing and defending epistemologies of universality and truth."

The state creates popular perceptions of right and wrong, good and evil, and works vigorously to reinforce and defend them. Ideological power is a formidable instrument in the creation of public support or condemnation. It provides a patina of legitimacy that serves to deflect much criticism. "Evil," as [criminal justice professor] Frank Hagan warns, "often gilds itself with an ideological gloss."

Why Professionals Serve Genocide

In closing, we must ask why do these professionals serve genocide so well?

First, we must recognize that many agree with the policies of destruction. Highly educated people are not immune to the biases and prejudices of the society in which they live.

Second, we must understand that many see cooperation as a vehicle to advancement and professional development. Just as scholars today often tailor their research based on opportunities, resources, and "hot" topics, so too do professionals in genocidal societies.

Third, it is important to note that science and bureaucracy are supposed to be amoral. Decisions and actions are supposed to be taken without reference to morality. Science is supposed to be objective, technical, rational, but not moral.

Fourth, we must also remember that the complicity is not necessarily deliberate. Genocidal states are adept at picking, choosing, and manipulating the theories and concepts of scholars.

Racial Discrimination by the Khmer Rouge Contributed to the Cambodian Genocide

Liai Duong

Liai Duong is a recent graduate of the Yale University Genocide Studies Program on whose comprehensive Web site appears the paper from which the following viewpoint was excerpted. Duong argues that racial discrimination by the Khmer Rouge led to the torture and deaths of thousands of Vietnamese, Chams, and Chinese. Racial stereotypes developed over years of compromised peace were used as tools to justify these genocidal acts. Although some of the violence perpetrated against these minority groups may not have been based in racist ideology, the deadly consequences are irrefutable.

In comparison to the Holocaust, it is more difficult to determine whether the Democratic Kampuchea government practiced racially discriminatory policies towards ethnic minorities during the Cambodian Genocide of 1975–79, because of the complexity of delineating what constitutes racial discrimination. Some scholars have disputed the existence of discriminatory policies towards ethnic minorities and have even argued that the ruling Khmer Rouge regime was innocent of genocide. This paper will examine whether the Khmer Rouge implemented racially discriminatory policies towards Cambodia's minority groups. Although Cambodia is composed of many ethnic groups, over 80% of its people are Khmer; only the larger minority groups with the most extensive documentation will be discussed in this paper: the Vietnamese, Chams, and Chinese. . . .

Liai Duong, "Racial Discrimination in the Cambodian Genocide," working paper for the Yale University Genocide Studies Program, 2006. www.yale.edu/gsp/publications/RacialDiscriminationInDK.doc. Reproduced by permission of the author.

Defining Racial Discrimination

The term "racial discrimination" is often liberally used without a clear understanding of its meaning. In order to determine whether the Khmer Rouge's policies towards ethnic minorities were racially discriminatory, it is important to present a clear definition of the term. For the purposes of this paper, the definition of racial discrimination will be taken from Article 1 of the International Convention of the Elimination of All Forms of Racial Discrimination, which defines this phenomenon as:

> any distinction, exclusion, restriction or preference based on race, colour, descent, or national or ethnic origin which has the purpose or effect of nullifying or impairing the recognition, enjoyment or exercise, on an equal footing, of human rights and fundamental freedoms in the political, economic, social, cultural or any other field of public life.[1]

When discussing racial discrimination it is also important to recognize the different forms in which it may occur. Often, people may associate racial discrimination with assumed biological superiority, meaning they believe that those who discriminate based on race do so because they feel they are inherently better than those they discriminate against. However, existence of a notion of superiority is not always necessary for racial discrimination to take place. As will be seen in the case of the Cambodia genocide, the Khmer Rouge's racially discriminatory policies did not necessarily arise out of a sense of biological supremacy. Instead, racial discrimination can arise from other motivating factors, such as politics, culture, and economics. When stereotypes surrounding these factors are applied to other groups, the threat of engaging in racial discrimination arises. For example, wealth was a factor that influenced how an individual would be treated by the Khmer

1. Ratified December 21, 1965. Entered into force January 4, 1969. http://www.unhchr.ch/html/menu3/b/d_icerd.htm.

Rouge. During their revolution, the Khmer Rouge initially divided the Cambodian population into two categories: "base people" (mostly peasants) and "new people" (mostly those who had lived in the cities).[2] The new people were typically treated the worse because they were forced to work harder and under worse conditions.[3] It will be shown how the Khmer Rouge's belief in the stereotype that all ethnic Chinese were economically affluent and were urban "new people," resulted in racially discriminatory policies directed towards them. Since the Khmer Rouge considered most Chinese a part of the wealthy class, the regime racially discriminated against the Chinese by treating them harsher than the Khmer. . . .

Khmer Rouge Racial Policies

Upon their victory in April 1975, the Khmer Rouge wanted to transform Cambodian society, seeking ways to attain national autonomy and fulfill notions of economic equality.[4] In order to achieve these goals, they imposed various policies, including forced evacuation of the urban population to collectivized rural labor communes. Over time, different types of policies would now be forced upon parts of the population, some of them with a stronger impact on minorities than on the ethnic Khmer majority. . . .

The Khmer Rouge sought to impose uniformity on the population by using "forced Khmerization," requiring minorities to abandon aspects of their distinct culture and to become "Khmer."[5] To facilitate this imposition of uniformity, the Khmer Rouge implemented policies that banned portions of cultures, such as minority languages and all religions, and they dispersed sectors of the population. . . .

2. Ben Kiernan, "The Ethnic Element in the Cambodian Genocide," in *Ethnopolitical Warfare: Causes, Consequences, and Possible Solutions*. Ed. Daniel Chirot and Martin E.P. Seligman (Washington, DC: American Psychological Association, 2001), 87.
3. Benedict Kiernan. *The Pol Pot Regime* (Chiang Mai: Silkworm Books, 1996), 288.
4. David P. Chandler. *A History of Cambodia* (Boulder: Westview Press, 2000), 209.
5. Elizabeth Becker. *When the War Was Over* (New York: Public Affairs, 1986), 243.

In addition to imposing uniformity, the Khmer Rouge adopted a policy of expulsion, in which they forced people out of the country. This policy was directed initially at the ethnic Vietnamese. The decision to expel the Vietnamese minority was a result of the poor political relationship between Cambodia and Vietnam, as well as the social stigma that had been projected onto the group. . . .

Furthermore, amongst all three minority groups, there is some evidence of a policy of extermination. There were frequent incidents that involved the Khmer Rouge killing many members of these minorities. Whether these killings were based on a conception of race has to be determined. Finally, the fourth type of policy encompasses all other types of discrimination. Examples include cases in which the Khmer Rouge prohibited members of all three minorities from holding political or military power.

The Vietnamese

Historically, tense relations between Cambodians and Vietnamese existed on both a social and political level. According to historian William E. Willmot, out of all the minority groups in Cambodia, the Vietnamese suffered from the most prejudice. On a social level, this prejudice against Vietnamese communities may be one result of the multiple historical Vietnamese invasions into Cambodia.[6] Furthermore, this acrimony may be a consequence of Vietnam's perceived past attempts to force its culture and institutions onto Cambodians.[7] . . .

Immediately after their victory, the Khmer Rouge sought to expel the Vietnamese from Cambodian territory. . . . In a matter of months, approximately 150,000 Vietnamese were driven from Cambodia.[8]

6. William E. Willmot. *The Chinese in Cambodia* (Vancouver: Publications Centre, Univ. of British Columbia, 1967), 35.

7. Chang, Pao-min. "Kampuchean Conflict: The Continuing Stalemate," *Asian Survey* 23 (1987): 748–763; p. 750.

8. Nayan Chanda. *Brother Enemy* (San Diego: Harcourt Brace Jovanovich, 1986), 16.

In mid-1976, the Khmer Rouge's policy towards the Vietnamese changed. Now, the regime allowed no more to leave the country.[9] Although the Khmer Rouge had expelled most Vietnamese from the country, not all had left. Some remained in the country for various reasons, such as the desire to stay with their Khmer spouses.[10] The regime massacred these ethnic Vietnamese who remained in Cambodia. The persecution of the Vietnamese coincided with the rising political conflict between Cambodia and Vietnam.[11] Specific orders were issued by the Khmer Rouge in April 1977 to arrest ethnic Vietnamese and anyone remotely associated with them, even those who simply knew their language.[12] As previously mentioned, even ethnic Khmer who were trained by Vietnamese military were executed. The extent of the massacres was significant. In May 1977 alone, approximately 420 Vietnamese in Kompong Chhnang province were executed.[13] Not only were Khmer Rouge officials active participants in the killings, but officials also forced Khmer spouses to kill their Vietnamese wives.[14]

It is apparent that the extermination and expulsion policies enacted towards the Vietnamese were forms of racial discrimination because these policies targeted a group based on race and at the very least, "impaired" their "exercise" of "fundamental freedoms." The Khmer Rouge did not force any other sector of the Cambodian population to leave the country. Perhaps if the regime had forced other groups to leave, then the presence of racial discrimination would have been less convincing, since everyone would have been subject to equal treatment. Instead, the Khmer Rouge allowed other minorities to stay within the borders and in some cases did not

9. Kiernan/*Pol Pot* 296. Interview, Kompong Trach.
10. Kiernan/*Pol Pot* 296.
11. Alexander Laban Hinton. *Why Did They Kill?* (Berkeley: University of California Press, 2005), 219.
12. Kiernan/*Pol Pot*, 297. From United States Department of State Interview.
13. Kiernan/*Pol Pot*, 297. *FBIS*, IV, 2 September 1977, p. H1, *Bangkok Post*, 1 September 1977.
14. Kiernan/*Pol Pot*, 296. Interview with Heng Samrin.

harm them if they had undergone "Khmerization." In contrast, the regime did not give the Vietnamese the option to remain. The extermination of the Vietnamese who remained in Cambodia was also racially discriminatory. The regime did not give ethnic Vietnamese the option to relinquish their ethnic identity as a mechanism for survival. One Khmer Rouge cadre stated, "If a person was ethnic Vietnamese, it was certain that they wouldn't survive. Once they were discovered, that was it."[15]

The Khmer Rouge's specific orders to exterminate the Vietnamese provide compelling evidence that the ethnic Vietnamese were singled out for persecution. Furthermore, the massacres that occurred revealed no signs of provocation aside from race. Since the Khmer had preexisting prejudices against the Vietnamese, transforming these prejudices into discriminatory acts might have taken place relatively easily. Additionally, race was a significant factor in determining who[m] to eradicate because even those remotely associated with the Vietnamese, including Khmer, were also killed. In this case, even being somewhat "tainted" by the Vietnamese, for instance knowing their language or being trained by their military, justified slayings of non-ethnic Vietnamese. The willingness to kill fellow Khmer reveals the determination of Khmer Rouge to eliminate any remote traces of the Vietnamese in their country. . . .

The Chams

The Chams are a minority group culturally distinct from the Khmer because of their language and Muslim faith, and the group was mainly composed of farmers and fishermen. In 1975, approximately 250,000 Chams lived in Cambodia.[16]

15. Hinton, 219.
16. Ben Kiernan. "The Demography of Genocide in Southeast Asia," *Critical Asian Studies* 35 (2003): 585–597.

Of this number, roughly 36%, or ninety thousand, would lose their lives by 1979 under the Khmer Rouge regime.[17]

In the case of the Chams, the Khmer Rouge enforced physical uniformity by prohibiting females from using their traditional headdress and by requiring them to cut their hair. They also required Chams to change their identity by forcing them to adopt Khmer names. However, perhaps what affected the Chams the most was the Khmer Rouge's decision to ban all religion—which included Islam, an intimate part of the Cham identity. To eradicate Cham religious practices, the Khmer Rouge forced them to violate their religion by consuming pork.[18] . . . Death was often the consequence for those who refused to obey the Khmer Rouge's orders. For instance, Cham survivor Lee Seyla witnessed the Khmer Rouge beating an estimated 10 Chams to death for merely refusing to eat pork.[19] Therefore, for Chams to increase their chances of survival, it was necessary for them to obey the regime and its policies. Not only did the Khmer Rouge take measures to eradicate all cultural identity in the population, but they also attempted to prevent the transmission of culture to future generations— essentially attempting to extinguish the Cham culture.

To help achieve this, the Khmer Rouge banned the use of all languages except for Khmer, and physically dispersed Cham families. . . . Physically dispersing the Chams into ethnic Khmer communities also helped to enforce uniformity and eradicate the race. . . . The dispersal of the Chams made it more difficult to practice their religion and, consequently, more difficult to pass their culture on to their children, thereby helping to slowly extinguish the culture.

As in the case of the Vietnamese, the Khmer Rouge also targeted Chams for execution. However, different factors con-

17. Kiernan/*Demography of Genocide*, 590.
18. Ysa Osman. *Oukoubah* (Phnom Penh: Documentation Center of Cambodia, 2002), 3. Interviews with Ly Khadijah, Math Dullah.
19. Lee Seyla. Interview by Nate Thayer. August 1984. No. 7. Transcripts provided by Ben Kiernan.

tributed to their deaths. Unlike the ethnic Vietnamese, many Chams rebelled against the regime's policies. These rebellions frequently resulted in the massacre of many Chams. . . .

As in the cases of the other minority groups, the Khmer Rouge banned Chams from engaging in political or military life. After the 1975 rebellion, Cham soldiers were demobilized.[20]

In 1976, Chams holding power, such as village chiefs and committee members, were forced to leave office in the Kor Subdistrict.[21] . . .

Because of the difficulties that forced assimilation can create, advocating uniformity seems inherently racial if only one group is forced to adopt aspects of a different culture. By not allowing diversity, the Khmer Rouge may have inadvertently racially discriminated against the Chams when they decided to make everyone adopt the Khmer culture. . . .

The Chinese

Like the Chams, the Chinese were subjected to the Khmer Rouge's desire to create national homogeneity. The Chinese were prohibited from communicating in their language and from practicing their religions. Additionally, the regime desired to create class uniformity by destroying the capitalist class, which was mainly composed of Chinese.[22] The Khmer Rouge's desire to create class uniformity resulted in harsher work conditions for the Chinese, whom the Khmer Rouge considered as "new people," not "base people."[23]

The Khmer Rouge also achieved uniformity by dispersing the Chinese. Although some of the ethnic Chinese were ini-

20. Ben Kiernan. Personal communication.
21. Ben Kiernan. "Orphans of Genocide: The Cham Muslims of Kampuchea under Pol Pot," *Bulletin of Concerned Asian Scholars* 20 (1988): 14. Information from Marcel Ner's "Les Musulmans de l'Indochine; Francaise," BEFEO XLI (1941), pp. 169, 175, 192, 194–195.
22. Becker, 228.
23. Sambath Chan. "The Chinese Community in Cambodia." *Searching for the Truth*, April 2003: 15–22; p. 20.

tially physically segregated from other races, they were eventually dispersed to live amongst ethnic Khmer. . . .

The emphasis on uniformity led to the elimination of all aspects of the Chinese ethnicity. In general, the Chinese who survived the genocide were those who had erased their ethnic attributes.[24]

There is substantial evidence of Chinese being targeted for execution; however, the reasons for the executions are not always clearly linked to race. According to El Yusof, "Chinese and Chams were preferentially selected [for execution] . . . though for the most part only those Chinese who were 'new people.'"[25] . . .

Given that the Khmer Rouge's treatment of the ethnic Chinese varied greatly and that other factors may have contributed to their persecution, can the policies towards the Chinese be considered racially discriminatory? According to [historian Ben] Kiernan there was no "racialist vendetta" against the ethnic Chinese, particularly when compared to the experiences of the Vietnamese and Chams, whom the Khmer Rouge killed even though many were clearly by no means part of the capitalist class.[26] The testimonies . . . from the ethnic Chinese do indicate that the Chinese may have had a better chance for survival under the Khmer Rouge regime if they were not associated with the capitalist class and were able to endure the rigorous labor. However, this is not to deny any elements of racial discrimination towards the Chinese. The Khmer Rouge's policies of enforced uniformity and of extermination directed towards the ethnic Chinese can still be seen as racially discriminatory.

In regards to uniformity, the act of eliminating an ethnic identity is itself inherently racially discriminatory. Like the Chams, the Chinese experienced the policy of coerced "same-

24. Becker, 250.
25. Kiernan. *Bulletin*, 17.
26. Ben Kiernan. "Kampuchea's Ethnic Chinese under Pol Pot: A Case of Systematic Social Discrimination." *Journal of Contemporary Asia* 16 (1986): 18–29; p. 20.

ness." However, it is likely that compared to the Chams, the Chinese did not have as difficult a time assimilating because their background in the Buddhist religion may not have conflicted with Khmer Rouge policies as directly as did the Islam of the Chams. For instance, the Chinese did not have to face problems such as avoiding pork or assembling enough individuals to complete their prayers. Yet if the degree to which the policies affected the Chinese may not have been as harsh, most Chinese still faced racial discrimination because they were forced to become "Khmer." . . .

In terms of the definition of racial discrimination, the Khmer Rouge relied on a stereotype that assumed all Chinese were economically wealthy. Based on this stereotype, their policies distinctively targeted the ethnic Chinese and impaired their fundamental freedoms and right to life (i.e., they were killed). Clearly, prejudices against race and wealth were not mutually exclusive, rather mutually reinforcing. The fact that the Khmer Rouge targeted the Chinese because they associated them with perceived negative stereotypes, demonstrates the presence of racial discrimination in the Khmer Rouge's policies. . . .

Race is a difficult subject to discuss because of its layers of complexity. This is particularly true in the case of the Cambodian genocide because of the multitude of factors that came into play when the Khmer Rouge generated their policies. Based on the definition of the phenomenon given by the International Convention of the Elimination of All Forms of Racial Discrimination, evidence suggests that there was racial discrimination in the Khmer Rouge's policies towards the ethnic Vietnamese, Chams, and Chinese. This racial discrimination is revealed in the different types of policies the Khmer Rouge directed at minorities, including the enforced imposition of uniformity, expulsion, extermination and discrimination. Although all three ethnic minorities experienced elements of racial discrimination, the degree to which they experienced it varied, with the ethnic Chinese experiencing the least effects of racially discriminatory policies. Regardless of whether or not the Khmer Rouge designed their policies to be racially discriminatory is irrelevant, because racial discrimination can be opportunistic or even inadvertent. Even though the Khmer Rouge's desire to harm ethnic minorities can be debated, the harmful effects of their discriminatory policies are incontestable. To the nation's misfortune, by enacting their political dreams, the regime quickly turned life into a tragic nightmare for many Cambodians who till this day continue to suffer from repercussions of this catastrophe.

Psychosocial Dissonance Contributed to the Cambodian Genocide

Alex Hinton

Alex Hinton is a professor of anthropology at Emory University in Atlanta and the author of a number of books about genocide, including Why Did They Kill?: Cambodia in the Shadow of Genocide. *In the following viewpoint he argues that psychosocial dissonance, or the conflict between an emotional, context-based version of the self and another concept of the self, greatly contributed to the Cambodian genocide. Prior to the genocide, the Cambodian people were described as gentle and kind, which contrasted with the violence of the genocide. To reduce this dissonance and make the Cambodian genocide participants into "agents of death," the Khmer Rouge modified existing cultural models and their contexts, Hinton argues.*

People often used to characterize Cambodia as a "gentle land" inhabited by nonviolent Buddhists who were always courteous, friendly, and ready with a smile. Beginning in the late 1960's, however, the country was rocked by socioeconomic unrest, civil war, intensive U.S. bombing, and, finally, social revolution. While around six hundred thousand of Cambodia's eight million inhabitants perished during these years, up to a million and a half people later died from disease, starvation, overwork, and execution during Democratic Kampuchea [the official name for Communist Cambodia] (1975–1979). Survivor accounts are replete with stories of how the Khmer Rouge [the Communist organization that ruled Cambodia] shot, bludgeoned, stabbed, and tortured legions of

Alex Hinton, "Agents of Death: Explaining the Cambodian Genocide in Terms of Psychosocial Dissonance," *Searching for the Truth*, vols. 31 and 32, July 2002. www.dccam.org/Tribunal/Analysis/Agents_Death.htm. Reproduced by permission.

their own countrypeople. This type of violence demands the attention of scholars. How could the seemingly "gentle" Cambodians come to commit such genocidal acts?

While other disciplines have addressed this challenging issue, anthropology has been remarkably silent on the topic of large-scale genocide, an omission that is particularly striking because anthropologists have demonstrated the ability to productively explain the roots of violence in other, non-genocidal contexts. To help to redress this deficiency, this essay will provide a psychosocial explanation of how people come to commit acts of genocide. . . .

Cognitive Dissonance in Individual Identity

[Social psychologist] Leon Festinger's original formulation of "cognitive dissonance" (CD) theory asserts that if a person holds two conflicting cognitions, she or he will be motivated to reduce the resulting state of psychological discomfort in a manner similar to drive reduction. Upon hearing a report that cigarette smoking is bad for their health, for example, many smokers will likely be motivated to reduce the resulting psychological discomfort/dissonance by: changing cognitions to make them more compatible (e.g., dismissing the research out of hand); circumspectly adding new cognitions that bridge the gap between the cognitive elements (e.g., finding information that indicates smoking is less dangerous than driving a car); or changing her or his behavior (e.g., stopping smoking). The stronger the "magnitude" of dissonance, the more a person will be motivated to reduce it.

This theory has generated a great deal of research, much of which indicates that cognitive dissonance is greatest when an individual has a behavioral commitment to one or both of the conflicting cognitions. Such experimental findings and a growing dissatisfaction with the vagueness of the original formulation of dissonance theory have led [psychologist] Elliot Aronson to assert that cognitive dissonance "is clearest and greatest when it involves not just any two cognitions but, rather, a cognition about the self and a piece of our behavior that violates that self-concept." Dissonance therefore arises in situations in which a person is confronted with behavioral expectations that conflict with this concept of the self. . . .

Psychosocial Dissonance from Cultural Pressure

Drawing on the aforementioned anthropological insights, we can now reformulate Aronson's theory of cognitive dissonance in the following manner. Cognitive dissonance arises when an (often culturally informed) emotionally salient cognition about the (culturally informed and context-dependent) self comes into conflict with another (often culturally informed) emotionally salient cognition that motivates behavior which violates that context-dependent self-concept. Psychosocial dissonance [PSD] is reserved for those cases in which an emotionally salient cultural model about the context-dependent self comes into conflict with another emotionally salient cultural model that violates that context-dependent self-concept. Thus, [in one case, a Pakistani woman named] Shamim experienced PSD when her parents' demands that she marry (i.e., the "good daughter" model that shaped her self-concept in familial interactions) began to conflict with her desire to achieve personal occupational goals (i.e., the "clever politician" model that informed her self-representations in the workplace). Whereas previously these contradictory models had been salient in different contexts, they began to overlap and caused PSD. PSD is thus a subset of CD, since all cultural models are cognitions, but not vice versa.

The degree of dissonance is a function of the emotional salience of a cognition. If being a "good daughter" was not particularly important to Shamim, she would only have experienced a small degree of PSD when her parents raised the subject of marriage. Because both the "good daughter" and the "clever politician" models were extremely important to her, however, Shamim experienced a great deal of PSD. People are motivated to reduce such dissonance because the cognitions in question establish goals that necessitate contradictory courses of action. In Shamim's case, her goal of getting married established a behavioral sequence that directly conflicted with her goal of advancing her career. I will examine the precise ways in which people attempt to reduce such dissonance in a later section. . . .

Many people have been struck by both the friendly demeanor of Cambodians and their ostensible lack of conflict in daily interactions. Given the harmonious atmosphere that is so prominent in everyday life, it is easy to be somewhat taken aback by the political violence that has characterized Cambodian history. Such violence illustrates the fact that while everyday communal life (i.e., relations with fellow members of a family, village, or organization) is frequently mediated by a high-level cultural model that fosters prosocial behavior, larger sociopolitical interactions (i.e., relations with an "enemy" in military activity, law enforcement, or national politics) are often informed by an extremely salient, yet potentially contradictory cultural model that promotes aggression. These two models, which I will hereafter respectively refer to as the "gentle ethic" and the "violent ethic," were significant in different interactional contexts and thus rarely came into conflict in pre-DK [Democratic Kampuchea] Cambodia. The conditions for PSD arose, however, when the violent ethic was legitimated in everyday communal interactions during DK. The unfortunate result was a situation in which acts of extraordinary violence took place. . . .

Festinger asserts a person can reduce cognitive dissonance by 1) changing given cognitive elements; 2) changing her or his behavior; 3) circumspectly adding new cognitions that bridge the gap between the dissonant cognitions; or 4) changing the situation in which given cognitions are salient. These dissonance reduction strategies can also, by extension, be used to reduce psychosocial dissonance. For example, a person experiencing PSD might 1) change one of her or his cultural models; 2) change the behavior that one of the cultural models entails; 3) add new, lower level schemas that bring the dissonant cultural models into consonance; and/or 4) alter the context in which the given cultural models are salient. This latter strategy is often difficult, since an individual rarely has the power to single-handedly change her or his environment. Totalitarian states, however, often do. While PSD reduction ultimately takes place on the individual level, a totalitarian state helps transform people into "agents of death" both by: 1) promoting an ideology that modifies existing cultural models; and 2) by changing the context in which the given models are salient.

The State Level Response

When the Khmer Rouge victoriously entered Phnom Penh [Cambodia's capital] on April 17, 1975, their first order of business was to evacuate Phnom Penh and the provincial capitals. This dispersal of the urban population was designed to control the citizenry, level class distinctions, create a strong labor base for the new agrarian, communist society, and weed out opposition. Leading military and civilian officials from the old government were rounded up and often executed. There was also a campaign to identify other potential traitors (e.g., teachers, students, bureaucrats, technical workers, and professionals). While some of these "class enemies" were killed, others were sent to be reeducated in special camps or through rural peasant life. At least one to two hundred thousand people died in this first wave of DK killing. Having dealt with these potential sources of opposition, the Khmer Rouge instituted a number of social and ideological reforms that served to facilitate genocide by altering the environment in which "agents of death" perpetrated their deeds.

The DK regime introduced a number of radical changes which undermined the "gentle ethic" that had previously characterized communal interactions. Whereas Cambodian life had formerly revolved around the village, cooperatives became the fundamental socioeconomic unit in DK. Economic and ecological conditions that had previously necessitated cooperation were rendered irrelevant. In contrast to the polite and friendly relations Cambodians had developed through kin/ friendship networks and years of communal association, interactions between "old people", "new people," soldiers, and local DK cadre in the cooperatives were often characterized by fear and suspicion. While people had previously observed patterns of etiquette that both regulated and diffused conflict, they were now told that everyone was equal and that obedience was due only to "the Organization" (*Ângkar*).

Intergroup harmony was further eroded by the destruction of Buddhism. Many of Cambodia's leading monks were executed immediately after the revolution, and the rest of the religious order was eventually forced to resume a secular life. Temples were often physically destroyed or desecrated, sacred texts were burned, and statuary was defaced. If a Cambodian child had previously received her or his earliest lessons on morality at the temple, she or he was now indoctrinated into an ideology that glorified revolutionary violence and blood sacrifice. Communism replaced Buddhism as the new "religion."

Whereas the family had previously constituted the primary social unit in Cambodian life, its bonds represented a threat to the DK regime. Consequently, the [Communist] Party attempted to diminish the importance of the family by eliminating its social and economic functions. Family members were systematically separated by housing restrictions, relocation, communal meetings, and long work hours in sexually segregated work teams. Such separation was part of a larger movement to redirect familial attachment to the state. In accordance with their official policy of egalitarianism and with their high valuation of children as the future of the revolution, the Party subverted patterns of etiquette that had traditionally governed interactions between family members. Indoctrination sessions informed children that they no longer had to act deferentially toward their parents. Mothers, fathers, children, and neighbors were all "comrades" (*mitt*) now.

As the gentle ethic was being undermined, the violent ethic was ideologically legitimated at the local level and began to inform everyday communal relations. While the leaders of the old regime had been eliminated and socioeconomic transformation begun, the DK regime was determined to bring the "spirit of combative struggle" to the cooperatives. Khmer Rouge ideology frequently employed the word *tâsou* ("to fight/ struggle bravely") to reference the warrior spirit. Everyone was expected to enlist in the revolutionary fight to "build and defend" (*kâsang neung karpear*) the country. The first battleground was the work site. Daily activity was reorganized along military lines. "Squads," "platoons," "companies," "battalions," and "divisions" of workers were sent to plant and harvest crops, to clear land, and to dig irrigation dams and canals. Like the military, this economic army was subject to strict discipline, harsh living conditions, and long work hours. . . .

The Individual Response

How do people become genocidal killers? As we have seen, one factor in this conversion process comes from a "state level response." In the case of Cambodia, the DK regime helped to reduce PSD by altering the environment (i.e., by undermining the gentle ethic and bringing the violent ethic to the local level) and by providing an ideology that could be used to modify these two cultural models (e.g., redefining the "enemy," ordering the execution of "traitors," promoting revolutionary violence). Ultimately, however, psychosocial dissonance occurs and is reduced on the individual level.

This "individual level response" will vary for each person. Based on her or his life history, an individual will need to take certain steps to become an "agent of death." Some people may just require a suitable environment to enact potentialities that they have already actualized. Others may have to undergo one or a series of transformations to become a killer. Still others may refuse to participate in a genocidal regime. Most genocidal killers probably fall into the middle category. . . .

In an attempt to erase hierarchical and class distinctions, the Khmer Rouge set out to divest the populace of "individualistic" qualities associated with a "capitalist" mentality. Personal property was abolished; work and eating were communized. Everyone was required to wear identical black garb, to cut their hair short, to adopt stereotypical patterns of "appropriate" speech and behavior, and to divest themselves of individualistic traits that precluded a proper revolutionary "consciousness." The ostensible goal was to create a homogeneous society in which the individual was subsumed by the state.

In reality, this homogeneous mass was divided along several lines. First, a clear distinction was made between the "true" Khmer who were a part of *Ângkar* and those who were its "enemies." Since *Ângkar* represented the people, any opposition to it was treasonous. Local level cadre were ordered to root out these "class enemies" who were attempting to subvert the Revolution. The first people to come under suspicion were "new" people: the urbanites and rural refugees who had been expelled from the cities and were suspect for having (in)directly supported the Lon Nol[1] forces which the Khmer Rouge had defeated. Their very exposure to foreign influence and imperialism suggested that new people were not "real Khmer" and thus enemies who should be treated in accordance with the violent ethic. This group was sharply distinguished from both Khmer Rouge cadre and soldiers and the "old"

1. Leader of the Khmer Republic, the opposing side of the Cambodian Civil War to the Khmer Rouge.

people who had lived under the Khmer Rouge during the difficult war years. From the very beginning, the relocated "new" people were "outsiders" who were treated more harshly.

In addition to being excluded from normal communal life, "new" people and other suspected enemies were subjected to dehumanizing practices. "New" people spoke of being crammed into trucks for many hours during later relocations. Often they had to defecate or urinate where they stood; the trucks didn't stop, even if someone died of suffocation. . . .

Such Khmer Rouge were indoctrinated into an ideology which instructed them to have no feeling for the enemy. As one cadre told me, "We were brainwashed to cut off our heart from the enemy, to be willing to kill those who had betrayed the revolution, even if the person was a parent, sibling, friend, or relative. Everything we did was supposed to be for the Party." This ideology of cutting off one's sentiment toward a now excluded and dehumanized "enemy" helped many Khmer Rouge reduce PSD both by redefining who was to be included in the new communist society and by creating a target group onto which they could project any anxiety-producing feelings. Because the revolutionary struggle continued in the cooperatives, Khmer Rouge cadre had little problem invoking the "violent ethic" to execute these hated enemies who were threats to the revolution, not "true" Khmer, and less than human. . . .

Attempts to Reduce Dissonance Increase Violence

How are people . . . converted into genocidal killers? As noted previously, the specific inputs required to turn someone into an "agent of death" will vary depending on that individual's life history. One, several, or all of the PSD reduction strategies discussed above may be pivotal in creating people who can commit acts of evil. These people will draw upon the "state level response" as they make their own "individual level response" to the PSD that arises when they kill. Such cognitive restructuring involves a dialectic in which complex processes interact to push the individual along the "continuum of destructiveness." The exclusion and devaluation of a group of individuals sets them outside of a given community. Dehumanization morally justifies the harm of these people. By using euphemisms and deflecting responsibility onto authority figures, any remaining culpability can be diffused. As people are harmed, the perpetrators become acclimated to violence. Desensitization makes the dehumanization of victims seem more normal.

Many Khmer Rouge would have experienced PSD when they were asked to kill people who had previously been members of their community (i.e., when the violent and gentle ethics came into conflict). These "agents of death" reduced their PSD in a number of ways. First, they changed these cultural models (i.e., they were able to do this because the DK regime effectively glorified violence and undermined the gentle ethic in the creation of the "killing fields"). Second, these actors changed their behavior (i.e., once they had killed, such violence became more routine). Third, Khmer Rouge cadre acted in an environment that had been dramatically altered (i.e., DK ideology not only legitimated but actually glorified the violent ethic in local level interactions). Finally, these individuals were able to add new, lower level schemas that made the larger cultural models more consonant (i.e., through dehumanization, the use of euphemism, moral justification, the deflection of responsibility). The result of this process of cognitive restructuring was the creation of "agents of death" . . . who could commit genocidal atrocities.

Religious Differences Contributed to the Bosnian Genocide

Michael Sells

Michael Sells is a professor of comparative religions at Haverford College in Pennsylvania. In the following viewpoint he argues that religious differences are often ignored as causes of genocide, or ethnic cleansing. In Bosnia, Catholics, Muslims, and Serbian Orthodox Christians committed violent acts against each other because of differing religious views, even though they were no different in racial or ethnic makeup. Religious differences were intensified following the breakup of Yugoslavia in the 1990s when identities were no longer based on nation-state affiliations.

The disintegration of the former Yugoslavia has been commonly attributed to ethnic, economic, political and social factors. Religion is commonly seen as not relevant to the conflict or as a disguise for deeper causes. Yet religion, in two senses, was a factor. First, victims were selected largely on the basis of their formal religious affiliation as Croat, Serb, or Muslim—that is, on the basis of their affiliation with Catholicism, Serb Orthodoxy, or Islam. In most cases there was no other distinguishing factor, such as appearance, language, or clothing. When the target identity was not apparent from personal names, then informants or records (such as voter registration lists) were needed to select victims for persecution. Some survivors have remarked, for example, that they had not viewed themselves as religious or even thought about their religious identity until they were singled out for persecution because of it: they discovered they had a religious identity only in the act of its being imposed upon them. This identity is

Michael Sells, "Crosses of Blood: Sacred Space, Religion, and Violence in Bosnia-Hercegovina: The 2002 Paul Hanly Furfey Lecture," *Sociology of Religion*, fall 2003.

commonly named ethnic rather than religious because it was handed down through the family, rather than being a matter of personal belief or religious practice. Because "religious" can refer to belief and practice, I am using the term "religion identity" rather than "religious identity" to refer to that identity, handed down through the family but connected to a religious tradition, that was the marker of difference in the Bosnia-Hercegovina (BH) conflict. The second role of religion in the tragedy centers on the institutions, symbols, rituals, and ideologies through which the violence was motivated and justified. This double aspect of religion is erased in discussions of ethnic hatreds or crimes of "ethnic cleansing" that are attributed to Serb or Croat nationalists. The crimes were committed by Serb and Croat nationalists who were at the same time Orthodox Christian and Catholic nationalists and the cleansing that took place was based upon religiously informed ideologies and constructions of difference.

Religion as an Ethnicity

The language of ethnicity to refer to the conflict in BH is grounded partially in the constitution of the post-WWII Yugoslavia, which on the one hand embraced several formal republics (Slovenia, Croatia, Bosnia-Hercegovina (BH), Serbia, Montenegro, and Macedonia) but also divided population by "narlon" (narod) Slovenians, Croats, Bosnian Muslims, Serbs, Montenegrins, and Macedonians. Non-Slavic populations were given the appelation of "nationality" (narodnost). The category of "Muslim" was created in the 1980's to offer Bosniacs and other Slavic Muslims a nationhood and thus a group enfranchisement that would be parallel to that of Bosnian Croats, and Serbs, but the term led to contradictions. Thus a Bosniac with a Muslim name but who was atheist and non-observant was of the "Muslim" nation while an Albanian Muslim who happened to be a believer and observant was designated "Albanian" with no reflection of Islam in the name of the nationality. Croats, Serbs, and "Muslims" (i.e. Bosniaks) the major elements that commonly viewed as constituting identity: they spoke the same language (that is, they understood each other when speaking, though for historical and political reasons they called the language by different names), shared a great many cultural features, and traced their descent to the same medieval South Slavic tribes. Because the term "nation" is used in a completely different manner in most English-speaking cultures, the English word "ethnicity" tends to be attached to the Yugoslav narod. The association of ethnicity with narod is reasonable, but can be misleading. We might, for example, refer to relations in South Asia violence between Punjabis and Gujaratis as ethnic, but not relations between Hindu Punjabis and Muslim Punjabis. Yet the distinction between Bosnian Serbs, Muslims, and Croats more closely parallels that between Hindu and Muslim Punjabis than it does between Gujaratis and Punjabis.

At issue here is not simply a matter of terminology. The language of ethnicity, when used to the exclusion of religion, shields a key factor in what has been called by the euphemism "ethnic cleansing," which was based solely and exclusively on distinctions of religion identity and was motivated and justified through a robust use of religion-based symbols and power. These symbols and this power were not cosmetic. Sacral architecture and sacred space are at the center of the struggle, both for those working for religious exclusion and those working for religious pluralism. The struggle over shrines illustrates in a particularly articulate way the exploitation and the deployment of the power of religion to advance particular visions of society and state in BH. . . .

Religious nationalism emerged in Serbia around the issue of Kosovo. In the Serbian province of Kosovo, the majority population of ethnic-Albanians began to demand more autonomy. Tensions with the Serb population grew. Serb bishops chimed that Kosovar Albanians were plotting to "ethnically cleanse" Serbs from Kosovo and—despite the radically secular basis of the Albanian autonomy movement—plotting an Islamic state in Kosovo as well. By 1986 Serb Orthodox bishops, church-affiliated journals, and intellectuals were charging Kosovar Albanians with a mass rape, annihilation of Serb shrines, and genocide. In response to the tensions in Kosovo, Slobodan Milosevic presented himself as the champion of Serbs and in 1987 used that role to seize control over crucial party and government institutions [eventually becoming president of Serbia in 1989]. . . .

Catholic Resurgence as Catalyst

"Ethnic cleansing" is commonly associated in the public mind with Serb nationalists. Certainly Serb political forces played the most public role in the breakup of Yugoslavia, and the Serb military carried out by far the largest and most sustained atrocities in BH as well as conquering 70 percent of the territory. In addition, the Serb Orthodox Church has called attention to itself through the militant role of its leadership in the conflict—exemplified by the close relationship of Serb bishops to the war-criminal Arkan, the massive Serb funeral processions of war criminals, and the attacks on the International Tribunal as an anti-Serb plot. True, Croatian President Franjo Tudjman had become notorious for his extreme nationalism and the crudity of his crude vision of Croatia as the buttress for Europe against the barbaric forces of the East, Orthodoxy and Islam. But the role of Catholicism in the "ethnic cleansing" of BH has been less acknowledged.

There are several reasons for this relative lack of acknowledgement. Tudjman and his allies in BH timed their attacks in such as way as to hide them partially behind the international outrage over the crimes of Serb forces. Croatia continued to assert, as an official position, its support of an independent BH while Tudjman and his BH allies made unofficial agreements with Serb nationalists to carve up BH between Serbia and Croatia. Beyond Tudjman's slyness in letting Serb nationalist aggression take the blame for the violence, there is another aspect that shields Catholic nationalism from view. As opposed to the Serb Orthodox leadership, which rivaled or exceeded Serb nationalist politicians in bellicosity, the Croat Catholic position was split. Catholic officials, both Franciscan and diocesan, were divided between religious pluralists and religious separatists. For those who looked at it seriously, the Orthodox Serb religious militancy of the Kosovo mythology and the 1989 Vidovdan ritual[1] were transparent. The enemies were named: Turkifiers (Slavic Muslims), Albanians, and Croats. The speeches and sermons bristled with talk of conflict. The Christ-killer implications of the Lazar[2] mythology were exploited systematically. But pronouncements from official Catholic sources, by contrast, did not focus on conflict-oriented identity formation and, for the most part, emphasized calls for love for peoples of all faiths.

After the death of Marshal Tito [Josip Broz, president for life of communist Yugoslavia] in 1989, Croat Catholic nationalism was galvanized around the now public campaign for the canonization of Cardinal [Aloysius] Stepinac. Stepinac was revered by Catholic Croat nationalists for his opposition to Tito's attempt to control the Church and for his persecution at the hands of the communist state. Stepinac is abhorred among Serbs and Serb clergy for his suspected support of the Ustashe[3] government of World War II and his refusal to take a strong public position in defense of Serbs, Jews, and others being persecuted by that regime. Resurgent Catholicism also

1. Vidovdan is a religious holiday in the Serbian and Bosnian Orthodox calendar, celebrated on June 28th, also a significant date commemorating the Battle of Kosovo in 1389 between the Ottoman Empire and Serbia.
2. Prince Stefan Lazar was a Serbian nobleman who fought during the Battle of Kosovo in 1389 between the Ottoman Empire and Serbia. He is also a saint in the Serbian Orthodox Church. His legend parallels that of Jesus Christ, in that he was betrayed, died, and was resurrected.
3. A Croatian nationalist organization put in charge of Croatia by the Axis Powers during World War II.

expressed itself architecturally. Even as the Cathedral of St. Sava was rising in Belgrade, the Franciscan Order was constructing a massive new church in the Croatian capital of Zagreb. . . .

The town of Stolac in southwestern Hercegovina offers a representative example of the attack. The HVO [Croatian Defense Union] militia launched a sudden attack on the Muslim inhabitants of Stolac, an ancient Bosnian town known for the richness of its cultural heritage and as the home of Bosnia's most important modern poet, Mak Dizdar. The August 1993 attack, away from any battle lines, was unprovoked by any military threat; indeed, its primary victims included Muslim men serving in the HVO, which for several months had been the only organized non-Serb force in the area. Both Muslim members of the HVO and those who had refused to join the HVO were seized, tortured and frequently killed. Survivors were sent to regional concentration camps where they were starved, deprived of water, and tortured in a pattern almost identical to that found in the Serb nationalist concentration camps. Women and children were driven on forced marches to areas under Bosnian government control. The elderly, very young, and weak sometimes perished on the march before the eyes of their mothers and daughters who could do nothing to help them. Once the town and surrounding villages had been cleansed of non-Catholics, non-Catholic sacral sites and other areas associated with Serb or Ottoman culture were destroyed . . .

Reconstruction as Continued Religious Violence

The effort to destroy the tangible and historical signs of non-Catholics in the area, and the memory that those signs and that population existed, is encountering further aspects of inverse causality. International teams of experts have volunteered to work continuously on reconstruction, peeling back through the history of each site, consulting or discovering written evidence, and reviving the traditional crafts and building skills necessary to construct the monuments in the traditional style. The rubble is examined when available and, even when it has been hidden in secret disposal sites, local Catholics in Stolac have volunteered information on those sites. The experts, graduate students, undergraduates, and scholars from various disciplines spread word of the destroyed shrines to all their circles personally, even as accounts of the monuments' reconstruction will make their way into various literatures. The goal is not to replicate an original structure, but to retrace and revive the layered heritage found in such sites. Each summer in Mostar an international symposium has been held on cultural heritage bringing the various groups of volunteers and experts together in a sustained manner.

Reconstruction includes inevitably the investigation of the original crime of destruction. In the case of the atrocities of ethnic cleansing, it is often difficult to recover the bodies of the victims. The vast majority of the thousands of men and women who were sexually abused or sexually tortured will not speak of their experience. But the shrines offer clear visual and tactile testimony. As the experts survey the site, they verify the methods of destruction and witness to the manner of destruction, refuting claims that the monuments were damaged by shelling, through collateral damage, during conflict between two armed forces, for example. Those who destroyed shrines were also identified in connection with other crimes, and the pattern of shrine destruction serves as a key test case in verifying other charges. The new triumph shrines placed by Croat nationalists are also a testimony. They are meant to sanctify the acts that were carried out on the sites where they are placed, as well as to inscribe a new historical, religious, and territorial text into the area. Yet they also provide a map of the atrocities and "ethnic cleansing" carried out from 1992 through 1995. By following the crosses and statues of the Virgin, one is able to trace the itinerary of the nationalist militias and the process of killing, expulsion, and destruction of the physical testimonies to the existence of the peoples removed.

The reconstruction process has strongly affected the position and morale of local residents. Once the reconstruction of the Careva [a Belgrade neighborhood] began in earnest, the psychology of the town was changed. The returning refugees, who had been afraid to leave designated ghettos, became more confident and began to walk throughout the town. Local Croats who had been afraid to show sympathy for or solidarity with their ex-neighbors also became less fearful. A number of local Catholics had contributed to the reconstruction, but had kept their names secret out of fear of the Catholic militants who control the area; most recently a Catholic contributor broke the silence and asked that his name be published. The choice to rebuild the mosque in traditional style also inhibits the attempt of well-funded Islamic missionary groups, largely from the [Persian] Gulf, to claim a hold on local Muslims by funding large, new structures cut off from local tradition. . . .

Religions in their ideological manifestations have traditionally been stronger at promoting an interior identity in opposition to the religious other than in affirming identity in affirmation of the other. After the cold war, religions have become central conduits of conflict. Their conflict-based paradigms have become repositories of power for the perpetuation of violence, claiming of territory, and rewriting of history through the rewriting of the textuality of the land itself. Those paradigms have run into the alternative vision supplied by those who refuse to identify their culture exclusively, but insist that identity as Bosnians and Hercegovinans is represented by the common civilization of which the shrines of various traditions are equally a part. Which vision of Bosnia-Hercegovina prevails may depend in part upon how what is called the world community—in this case, historians, human rights workers, international development officials, policy makers, and potential pilgrims to Medjugorje [a Catholic parish in BH reported to have been the site of apparitions of the Virgin Mary]—to read the language of shrines.

Extreme Poverty Led to the Rwanda Genocide

Paul Magnarella

Attorney and anthropologist Paul Magnarella is chair of the Peace Studies Program at Warren Wilson College in Asheville, North Carolina. In the following viewpoint he argues that while social and political imbalances contributed to the 1994 Rwanda genocide, extreme poverty was the predominant factor that led to the killings. Conflicts between the amount of land available for farming and the growing population caused famine. According to Magnarella, the Rwandan government attempted to solve these problems by encouraging the elimination of the Tutsis and Hutu sympathizers rather than by addressing the problems through social and economic reforms.

In 1994, Rwanda erupted into one of the most appalling cases of mass murder the world has witnessed since World War II. Many of the majority Hutu (about 85% of the population) turned on the Tutsi (about 12% of the population) and moderate Hutu, killing an estimated total of 800,000 people. Since genocide is the most aberrant of human behaviors, it cries out for explanation. . . .

Food-People-Land Imbalance

Hutu and Tutsi lived together relatively peacefully prior to the mid-nineteenth century, a time when their total population was comparatively low (probably less than two million, versus over seven million in 1993) and land supply for both Hutu farmers and Tutsi cattle grazers was ample. With rapid population growth in the twentieth century, the situation changed.

Paul Magnarella, "Explaining Rwanda's 1994 Genocide," *Human Rights and Human Welfare*, vol. 2, issue 1, 2002. Reproduced by permission of University of Denver's Graduate School of International Studies.

Rwanda was faced with a critical food-people-land imbalance. Throughout the twentieth century, Rwanda's people had placed tremendous pressure on the land. As early as 1983, when Rwanda had 5.5 million people and was the most densely populated country in all of Africa, expert observers warned that food production could not keep up with basic needs. By 1993, one year before the genocide, the population had climbed to 7.7 million without any substantial improvement in agricultural output even though an estimated 95 per cent of the gainfully employed population was engaged in agriculture. To the contrary, food production had been seriously hampered by periodic drought, overgrazing, soil exhaustion and soil erosion. In the years leading up to the genocide there had been a marked decline in kilocalories per person per day and overall farm production. Famines occurred in the late 1980s and early 1990s in several parts of the country. Hunger was endemic. Rwandan youth faced a situation where many (perhaps most) had no land, no jobs, little education, and no hope for a future. Without a house and a source of livelihood, they could not marry.

Because of their historically different modes of ecological adaptation—Hutu horticulture and Tutsi cattle pastoralism—within the context of a society over 90 per cent agrarian, a rapidly growing rural population, no significant employment alternatives, and diminishing food production and consumption per capita, the Hutu and Tutsi became "natural competitors." Those Tutsi still engaged in cattle pastoralism wanted open ranges to graze their herds. In direct opposition, landless Hutu wanted those very lands, marginal as they may have been for agriculture, to build homesteads on and to farm.

By flight or death of more than half of Rwanda's Tutsi population from the early 1960s to 1973, vast tracts of land in the eastern region were freed up for Hutu settlement and cultivation. The political elites exploited these developments, which appeared to prove that Hutu farmers could have sufficient land if the Tutsi were eliminated. By the mid-1980s, population increases had again outstripped the amount of cultivable land. Farmers' attempts to increase food production by double- and triple-cropping their dwindling plots resulted in soil exhaustion. Foreign technical experts could do little to help farmers; the problem was the increasing imbalance of the land:people ratio. The 1990–93 war with the RPF [Rwandan Patriotic Front, a Tutsi refugee group,] contributed further to the devastation of Rwanda's economy. It displaced thousands of farmers in the north, thereby causing reductions in food and coffee production. It closed Rwanda's main land route to Mombassa [Kenya] and the outside world. It destroyed Rwanda's small tourism industry, which had become the third major foreign exchange earner.

Eliminating the Tutsi

There were few employment alternatives to farming. The country's major employer was the government. In the late 1980s, the central government was employing 7,000 people and the local governments 43,000. By law, only nine per cent of these employees could be Tutsi. Eliminating the Tutsi would open up 4,500 more government jobs for Hutu. Because the country had no social security program, the thousands of unemployed young people who entered the job market each year lived on the very margins of survival. Many became easy subjects for recruitment and manipulation. Two of the Hutu militias responsible for the mass killing were the *Interahamwe* and the *Impuzamugambi*. Both tended to recruit mostly among the poor, who hoped to benefit economically from the genocide.

[President Juvenal] Habyarimana had adamantly refused to allow Tutsi refugees back into the country, insisting that Rwanda was too small and too crowded to accommodate them. Some Rwandans believed that mass exterminations were necessary to wipe out an excess of population and bring numbers into line with the available land resources. However, economic conditions alone do not explain the mass murders. The strategies of Hutu leaders must also be taken into account. In this poor country, regional Hutu elites vied with each other to acquire the economic resources—especially tax revenue and foreign aid—that the reins of political power controlled. Their common plan involved marginalizing the educated Tutsi to eliminate any domestic competition from them and demonizing all Tutsi so as to dupe poor Hutu, the vast majority of the population, into believing that the elites protected them and represented their interests. With the Tutsi sidelined, Hutu regional elites competed with each other.

The Government and the Economy

Rwanda's poor economy rests on peasant subsistence agriculture. The governing elite could extract only limited surplus value directly from the peasant masses. In addition to taxes, the governing elite had two other potential sources of enrichment: skimming export revenues and foreign aid. During the late 1980s and early 1990s, the three sources of export earnings—coffee, tea, and tin—all declined. Coffee export receipts declined from $144 million in 1985 to $30 million in 1993. Hence, export revenues declined, government budgets were cut, and the only remaining source of enrichment was foreign aid. Those who could benefit from it had to be in positions of political power. Consequently, elite Hutu engaged in a fierce competition for control of the rapidly shrinking economy. But, rather than negotiate in earnest with the RPF, Habyarimana chose to increase the size of his armed forces (from 5,000 in 1990 to 30,000 in 1992), thereby diverting scarce resources from needed food imports, health care, and education.

The rule of dominant persons does not depend on political or economic power alone, but on persuading the ruled to accept an ideology that justifies the rulers' privileged positions and convinces the ruled that their best interests are being protected. From the 1960s until 1994, the ideology promoted by the Hutu ruling elite was as follows: Tutsi were foreign invaders, who could not really be considered as citizens. The Hutu had been the "native peasants," enslaved by the aristocratic invaders: they were now the only legitimate inhabitants of the country. A Hutu-controlled government was now not only automatically legitimate but also ontologically democratic. This political ideology validated both the persecution of Tutsi and the autocratic rule by some elite Hutu.

As for its economic ideology, the government promoted the idea that the Hutu "holy way of life" was farming. It strictly limited rural migration to the city. People could not change their residences without government permission, and that was rarely given. Consequently, the government made no attempt to significantly diversify the economy so as to create a viable nonagricultural sector or to limit population growth (except by killing and expelling Tutsi). . . .

The authorities told common Hutu that the Tutsi RPF and all those who sided with them were demons who had to be eliminated. In addition to relieving fear of supposed Tutsi evil, eliminating the demons also earned material rewards (land, cattle, loot) for the killers.

Murder as a Solution

In conclusion, the *sine qua non* [indispensable condition] of the Rwandan genocide was the increasing imbalance in land, food, and people that led to malnutrition, hunger, periodic famine, and fierce competition for land to farm. Rwanda's leaders chose to respond to these conditions by eliminating the Tutsi portion of the population as well as their Hutu political rivals. They employed the weapons of indoctrination to convince the Hutu masses that this strategy was right. However, they failed to employ the kinds of demographic and economic policies that would have addressed these problems in a peaceful and more effective way. These policies would have included birth control, economic diversification into non-agrarian sectors, requests for significant foreign food aid, sincere negotiation with the RPF, and attempts at a regional solution to the refugee problem. . . .

I would argue that the ultimate causes of the Rwandan genocide were the country's economic plight, caused in large part by the world economy and Rwanda's growing imbalance in land, food, and people that led to malnutrition, hunger, periodic famine, and fierce competition for land to farm. The proximate causes were the political indoctrination that demonized the Tutsi and convinced many Hutu that Tutsi elimination was the country's economic and political remedy.

Favoritism by the Roman Catholic Church Led to the Rwanda Genocide

British Church Newspaper

In the years following the 1994 Rwanda genocide, a number of Roman Catholic Church leaders were charged with committing crimes against humanity. While some of them were acquitted, many of them, including a high-ranking nun and several priests, were convicted. In the following viewpoint a correspondent for the British Church Newspaper, *a Bristol-based Protestant newspaper, argues that Roman Catholic Church leaders created divisiveness between the two major Rwandan ethnic groups, the Hutus and the Tutsi. According to the author, some of the "White Fathers," as they were called, even carried out genocidal acts against Tutsis in their own parishes.*

Events and media coverage of the 10th anniversary of the Hutu massacres of 800,000 Tutsis in the spring of 1994 have strangely omitted the role of the institution largely responsible for the genocide—the Roman Catholic [RC] Church. Its role may be compared to its role in supporting the Nazis in the 1930s.

When German colonialists arrived in numbers in Rwanda-Burundi in the 1870s, they found, for Africa, a remarkably well-ordered society. The Tutsis, not an ethnic group as such but based on the Nyiginya tribe, were dominant. They were mostly cattle owners, holding power in the all important 'central court' and its satellite institutions, while the Hutu were mostly peasant farmers. But Hutu farmers could move into the Tutsi elite on merit, with Hutu chiefs playing a significant role in society.

British Church Newspaper, "Genocide of the Tutsis: The Role of the Roman Catholic Church," *British Church Newspaper*, April 16, 2004. Reproduced by permission of European Institute of Protestant Studies.

From the 1880s onwards, Belgian Roman Catholic missionaries from the Vatican's 'White Fathers Order' increased their influence in the area, and in the 1919 Versailles settlement after World War I, Rwanda became a League of Nations 'Trust Territory' under Belgian control.

Darwinian Evolutionary Theory

The 'White Fathers' consolidated their influence. Darwinian evolutionary and racial theories were then in full flow. The 'Fathers' developed a bizarre racist theory to explain the relatively well-ordered African society they were dealing with, the so-called 'Hamitic hypothesis'. This proclaimed that 'civilised' African societies emanated from an invasion of 'Hamites' who originally settled in Ethiopia.

Rwandan history was effectively rewritten by RC academics and Belgian colonial administrators. The Tutsi were Hamites, descended from Ham [son of Noah] whilst the Hutus were of inferior stock and destined to be treated like Bantu serfs, whilst a small group of hunter-gatherers and potters, the Twa, were regarded as 'aboriginal pygmoids'—supposedly remnants of an earlier stage of human evolution.

The result was that only Tutsi were now given places of responsibility in Rwanda; their existing powers and privileges increased greatly. Understandably, Hutu resentment grew.

Young Papal Missionaries

After World War II, the influence of the White Fathers Order diminished as a new wave of young Papal missionaries came over from Belgian seminaries. They brought with them 'social justice' theories that were now being developed by the Vatican to promote RC influence in third world countries. These mostly Flemish priests identified with the by-now oppressed Hutu majority, took up their cause, and gradually forced the Tutsis to relinquish their grip on the country. One result was a Hutu uprising in 1959 which led to 10,000 Tutsis being killed and over 100,000 being driven abroad.

Three years later, Gregoire Kayibanda, Secretary to Monsignor Vincent Nsengiyuma, Rwanda's Archbishop, became first President of an independent Rwanda, having earlier founded the racial supremacist 'Parme Hutu' party. Now the Tutsi were seen by RC thinkers as 'invaders' from Ethiopia and the RC Church orchestrated calls for the Tutsi to be 'sent back home'.

Tutsi 'Cockroaches'

A notable event was the disgraceful letter sent in 1972 to the Archbishop by a group of eleven Hutu RC priests and religious leaders, referring to the Tutsi as 'inyenzi' (cockroaches)—a word used frequently by Hutu killers in 1994. Referring to the 1959 massacres, the letter read: "After the defeat of the counter-revolutionaries, the inyenzi, one would have thought that reasonable people, consecrated to God's service, would bow down before the irreversible victory of the people. The Hutu seem to have fallen asleep on the laurels of victory while the Tutsis are working very hard in order to again become masters of events. How long can we allow our Tutsi brothers to make fools of us?" One of the letter's authors, Andre Havugimana, later rose to high office in the Rwandan RC Church.

The year following that letter, the RC Church publicly endorsed the purge of Tutsis from schools, colleges and the civil service. Abuses and occasional massacres of Tutsis were the inevitable result of this persecution. In 1992, Hassan Ngeze, a journalist working for the extremist Hutu party, published a Hutu manifesto, titled 'The Hutu Ten Commandments'. Commandment No. 8 was "Stop having mercy on the Tutsis".

Rome, the USA and the Genocide

The events leading up to the genocide in April 1994 were, according to many experts, planned and co-ordinated by RC church leaders and politicians in conjunction with Hutu racial supremacists and United States Ambassador David Rawson.

Rawson's previous post had been in Somalia, where he had spent millions of dollars providing US military weapons to the discredited Barre regime. That was followed by an ignominious US exit from Somalia as that country descended into chaos.

A key US role in the Rwandan massacres was to deny that genocide was taking place, since under international law that would have 'obliged' the UN and the international community to intervene. Instead, they claimed there were merely 'individual acts of genocide'. They also actively frustrated UN attempts to send troops to Rwanda.

In a 1999 *Guardian* [Manchester, UK] article, Chris McGreal wrote of the failure of the RC church to prevent the bloodshed: "It failed because it claims four out of five Rwandans as adherents, yet it made little effort to influence the killers. That failure continues today through denial and evasion over its responsibility for the genocide".

Rome, the Ecumenists and the Massacre

A number of RC priests actively participated in the genocide of the Tutsi, including Augustin Misago, charged [and acquitted] with dispatching children to serve in the Hutu militia. In one incident, dozens of unarmed Tutsis were slaughtered in a RC church. Misago said: "They brought it on themselves by hiding guns". Two years later, a human rights group, who investigated RC participation in the massacres, wrote to the Pope saying: "One is struck by the persistent wish to exonerate the RC hierarchy and the institution at any price". It is sad to record that some compromising, ecumenical, once Protestant religious institutions also 'turned a blind eye to the massacres.

[In 2004,] Prime Minister [of the UK] Tony Blair announced that he would urgently bring forward legislation to introduce identity cards. Just as the identification of the Jews on local authority registers in Holland in the 1930s enabled Hitler's men to rapidly identify and round up Jews there in

1940, it is salutary to note that the Catholic-inspired racial ideology of the 1920s and 1930s required all Rwandans to carry papers identifying them as either Hutu, Tutsi or Twa. This made the job of the Hutu mass-murderers, whose efforts at one time led to 40,000 Tutsi bodies floating down to Lake Victoria, all the easier.

The Japanese Military Committed Genocide in Nanking, China

The Bill of Rights in Action

In the following viewpoint the Bill of Rights in Action, *a publication of the Constitutional Rights Foundation, presents an argument that the Nanking Massacre, also known as the "Rape of Nanking," was a genocide carried out by vengeful Japanese soldiers. The author asserts that during a six-week period at the end of 1937 and the beginning of 1938, Japanese soldiers tortured and murdered scores of Chinese men, women, and children. A number of Japanese military leaders were convicted and executed for committing crimes against humanity during the Tokyo Trials conducted by the International Military Tribunal for the Far East in 1948.*

At the beginning of World War II, Japanese soldiers committed many atrocities against POWs [prisoners of war] and civilians in Nanking, China. After the war, a war crimes trial focused on who was responsible for these acts.

For much of human history, the idea of "war crimes" did not exist. Victorious armies often slaughtered defeated enemy soldiers and civilians as well. About a hundred years ago, however, most major nations in the world began to agree on certain "rules of war."

In 1899 and 1907, at a city called The Hague in the Netherlands, the world powers agreed to prohibit the killing or mistreatment of prisoners of war and civilians. In effect, these Hague Conventions made it illegal under international law for soldiers and their commanding officers to carry out acts that came to be called "war crimes."

The Bill of Rights in Action, "The 'Rape of Nanking,'" *The Bill of Rights in Action*, vol. 8, No. 3, summer 2002. Reproduced by permission of Constitutional Rights Foundation.

Going to War with China

Japan was one of the nations that signed and ratified the Hague Conventions. Japan was fast becoming a modern and industrialized country with a military force patterned after those of Europe. Following the example of European colonial powers, Japan went to war against China in 1894 to gain control of some Chinese trading ports. In 1905, Japan defeated Russia in a war over possession of ports in the Chinese territory of Manchuria. It was the first Asian nation to defeat a European power.

By the early 1930s, Japanese military and political leaders believed that it was Japan's destiny to acquire China. They thought that Japan's economic survival depended on control of Chinese agricultural lands and other resources.

Meanwhile in China, revolutionaries had overthrown the last emperor and were trying to unify the country under the leadership of Chiang Kai-shek. The Japanese viewed these events as a threat to their plans for dominating China as a colony. In response, Japan seized all of Manchuria in 1931.

In 1937, two years before [Adolf] Hitler started World War II in Europe, and four years before Japan attacked Pearl Harbor, the Japanese launched another invasion of Chinese territory. This time, they occupied the Chinese capital city, Peking (now spelled Beijing). In addition, they sent a major force to attack Shanghai, China's largest city (located near the mouth of the Yangtze River).

Heading to Nanking

Outside Shanghai, the Japanese, under the command of General Matsui Iwane, met heavy resistance from Chiang Kai-shek's army. The battle raged on for several months, killing thousands on both sides. Finally, in early November 1937, Chiang ordered his army to retreat 250 miles inland along the Yangtze River to Nanking (now spelled Nanjing), the new Chinese capital. General Matsui's troops pursued the Chinese, who soon began to flee in panic.

Although Matsui issued orders forbidding mistreatment of the Chinese people, Japanese soldiers felt vengeful. They had endured fierce fighting in the battle for Shanghai. Japanese troops executed many Chinese soldiers who had surrendered. They also killed draft-age men, whom they suspected of being enemy soldiers disguised as civilians. Because the Japanese military high command in Tokyo had failed to establish an adequate supply system for their troops, soldiers began stealing food from the countryside. This led to further abuses of Chinese civilians.

The Fall of Nanking

As Japanese troops moved closer to Nanking, Chiang Kai-shek, Chinese government officials, and many civilians left the city. Chiang, however, ordered his generals and about 100,000 soldiers to remain and defend the Chinese capital.

In early December 1937, Japanese air strikes and artillery bombarded Nanking. In battles outside the city, Chinese troops proved no match for the Japanese.

The Japanese demanded that if the Chinese did not surrender Nanking, "all the horrors of war will be let loose." Chiang Kai-shek refused to permit the surrender of the capital, but finally ordered the defenders to evacuate. Panic gripped the city. Chinese soldiers and civilians desperately tried to flee Nanking before the Japanese arrived.

When the Japanese surrounded Nanking on December 12, they trapped tens of thousands of Chinese soldiers and about 200,000 civilians in the city. Although most foreigners had fled Nanking, a group of about 25 American and European businessmen, doctors, nurses, college professors, and Christian missionaries remained. In the weeks leading up to the fall of Nanking, they formed a committee to organize a two square mile "International Safety Zone" within the city.

The purpose of the Safety Zone was to shelter and protect the Chinese civilians still living in Nanking. The Safety Zone

Committee elected an unlikely leader—John Rabe. He was a German businessman who also headed the Nazi Party in Nanking. Even so, Rabe worked tirelessly and put his life in danger to shelter and save the lives of many Chinese.

When Japanese troops finally marched into Nanking on December 13, 1937, thousands of civilians crowded into the Safety Zone. The Safety Zone Committee decided to also admit stranded Chinese soldiers. The Japanese never fully agreed to honor the Safety Zone, but allowed the committee of foreigners to feed and house the people seeking refuge there.

The Execution of POWs

Thousands of Chinese soldiers had surrendered before the Japanese entered Nanking. Once in the city, Japanese troops rounded up any Chinese soldiers they found in house-to-house searches and in the Safety Zone.

Since defeated Chinese soldiers often exchanged their military uniforms for civilian clothes, the Japanese also arrested many draft-age males not in uniform. Undoubtedly, this group included many civilians—policemen, firemen, city employees, hospital workers, servants, and others.

The Japanese faced the problem of what to do with these POWs. A feeling of vengeance against the Chinese ran strong among Japanese troops. The Japanese had difficulty feeding their own soldiers, let alone tens of thousands of Chinese POWs. The Japanese also saw the POWs as a security risk. They didn't have a camp to hold them. They thought the POWs threatened the safety of the Japanese soldiers as well as a planned victory parade in Nanking led by General Matsui.

The Japanese army had no clear POW policy. Division commanders in Nanking took matters into their own hands and ordered the execution of the POWs under their control. The Japanese shot some by firing squad and bayoneted others to death. In some cases, the Japanese lined up POWs in groups from 100–200 on the banks of the Yangtze and machine-gunned them. Some Japanese officers used their swords to behead POWs.

About 40,000 Chinese POWs and civilian draft-age men probably perished within a week or so. The Japanese had committed the first major war crimes of World War II. But the worst was yet to come.

Cases of Disorder

Atrocities (brutal acts) against the people of Nanking began as soon as Japanese troops entered the city. Unlike the POW executions ordered by Japanese army division commanders, most atrocities against Nanking's civilians were criminal acts done by undisciplined soldiers.

Japanese soldiers beat people, robbed them at gunpoint, and murdered them almost randomly. The soldiers stabbed people with bayonets, mutilated them with knives, and even ran over them with tanks. The soldiers vandalized, looted, and burned public buildings and private homes. They even destroyed animals for no reason.

For more than a month, Japanese soldiers roamed the city hunting for women to rape. The soldiers raped women and girls on the street, in stores, and in homes before horrified family members. The victims ranged in age from 10 to over 60. Even pregnant women were sexually assaulted. Gang rapes and kidnappings for the purpose of rape occurred. Raped women were sometimes mutilated or killed. The rapists killed children and even infants simply because they got in the way. Japanese soldiers frequently invaded the International Safety Zone in search of women. On several occasions, John Rabe, the leader of the Safety Zone Committee, stopped sexual assaults by displaying his Nazi swastika armband. The soldiers did not want to get into trouble with a country that they knew was a friend of Japan.

During the weeks of terror in Nanking, the Safety Zone Committee sent letters and eyewitness reports of the atrocities to Japanese diplomats, hoping they could stop the rampaging soldiers. Called "Cases of Disorder," these reports detailed what was happening to the people of Nanking.

The Safety Zone Committee recorded this account of a case that took place on January 15, 1938:

> Many Japanese soldiers arrived [at a Chinese temple], round[ed] up all the young women, chose 10, and raped them in a room at the temple. Later the same day a very drunken Japanese soldier came, went into one room demanding wine and women. Wine was given, but no girls. Enraged, he started to shoot wildly, killing two young boys, then left. . . .

Who Was Responsible?

General Matsui was the overall commander of Japanese military operations in Central China. Headquartered in Shanghai, he did not personally witness the terrible events that unfolded in Nanking. A few days after Japanese forces occupied the Chinese capital, however, Matsui entered the city to lead a victory parade. Learning of the atrocities that Japanese soldiers were committing, he ordered that "anyone who misconducts himself must be severely punished."

After General Matsui returned to Shanghai, the atrocities against the people continued in Nanking. Army division commanders did little to stop them.

In Shanghai, General Matsui issued new orders, stating that the "honor of the Japanese Army" required punishment for the illegal acts of soldiers. Again, the Japanese commanders in Nanking were unwilling or unable to control their troops. Only after Matsui returned to Nanking in early February 1938, six weeks after the fall of the city, did order and discipline improve among the occupying troops.

Even today, great controversy arises over the number of victims in the "Rape of Nanking." Official Chinese figures put the number of fatalities at 300,000. Some in Japan deny the massacre took place. But today Japanese textbooks, which for years did not mention Nanking, estimate that 200,000 were killed. The latest research indicates that Japanese troops probably killed at least 50,000 to 100,000 POWs and civilian men, women, and children. Many thousands more were rape victims and others who were injured but survived.

War Crimes on Trial

Who, then, was responsible for these atrocities?

As they did at Nuremberg, Germany, the victorious Allies conducted war crimes trials in several Asian nations after the war. At Nanking, a war crimes tribunal convicted and hanged three Japanese army lieutenants for beheading hundreds of Chinese POWs. The Nanking tribunal also tried and executed one Japanese general who commanded troops in Nanking.

In Tokyo, more than two dozen Japanese political and military leaders also faced a war crimes tribunal. General Matsui was indicted for "deliberately and recklessly" ignoring his legal duty "to take adequate steps to secure the observance and prevent breaches" of the laws of war (the Hague Conventions). In his defense, General Matsui said that he never ordered the POW executions. He also argued that he had directed his army division commanders to discipline their troops for criminal acts, but was not responsible when they failed to do this.

The majority of the judges at the Tokyo tribunal ruled that General Matsui was ultimately responsible for the "orgy of crime" because, "he did nothing, or nothing effective to abate these horrors."

A dissenting judge, Radhabinod Pal from India, disagreed with the majority. He concluded that the commander-in-chief must rely on his subordinate officers to enforce soldier discipline. "The name of Justice," Pal wrote in his dissent, "should not be allowed to be invoked only for ... vindictive retaliation." American military authorities hanged General Matsui on December 27, 1948.

The Ottoman Government Committed Genocide Against the Armenians

Rouben Paul Adalian

Rouben Paul Adalian is the director of the Armenian National Institute, a Washington, D.C.–based, nonprofit organization dedicated to the study and affirmation of the Armenian genocide. In the following viewpoint he argues that the Ottoman state, once a powerful empire that in 1923 became the Republic of Turkey, carried out genocide against the Armenian people in the hopes of creating a new Turkish empire. Thousands of Armenian men, women, and children were deported from their homeland and into the Syrian desert. According to the author, many of them were murdered or starved to death along the way.

In April 1915 the Ottoman government embarked upon the systematic decimation of its civilian Armenian population. The persecutions continued with varying intensity until 1923 when the Ottoman Empire ceased to exist and was replaced by the Republic of Turkey. The Armenian population of the Ottoman state was reported at about two million in 1915. An estimated one million had perished by 1918, while hundreds of thousands had become homeless and stateless refugees. By 1923 virtually the entire Armenian population of Anatolian Turkey had disappeared.

Before the Genocide

The Ottoman Empire was ruled by the Turks who had conquered lands extending across West Asia, North Africa and Southeast Europe. The Ottoman government was centered in

Rouben Paul Adalian, "Armenian Genocide," www.armenian-genocide.org, November 8, 2006. Reproduced by permission of the Armenian National Institute.

Istanbul (Constantinople) and was headed by a sultan who was vested with absolute power. The Turks practiced Islam and were a martial people. The Armenians, a Christian minority, lived as second-class citizens subject to legal restrictions which denied them normal safeguards. Neither their lives nor their properties were guaranteed security. As non-Muslims they were also obligated to pay discriminatory taxes and denied participation in government. Scattered across the empire, the status of the Armenians was further complicated by the fact that the territory of historic Armenia was divided between the Ottomans and the Russians.

In its heyday in the sixteenth century, the Ottoman Empire was a powerful state. Its minority populations prospered with the growth of its economy. By the nineteenth century, the empire was in serious decline. It had been reduced in size and by 1914 had lost virtually all its lands in Europe and Africa. This decline created enormous internal political and economic pressures which contributed to the intensification of ethnic tensions. Armenian aspirations for representation and participation in government aroused suspicions among the Muslim Turks who had never shared power in their country with any minority and who also saw nationalist movements in the Balkans result in the secession of former Ottoman territories. Demands by Armenian political organizations for administrative reforms in the Armenian-inhabited provinces and better police protection from predatory tribes among the Kurds only invited further repression. The government was determined to avoid resolving the so-called Armenian Question in any way that altered the traditional system of administration. During the reign of the Sultan Abdul Hamid (Abdulhamit) II (1876–1909), a series of massacres throughout the empire meant to frighten Armenians and so dampen their expectations, cost up to three hundred thousand lives by some estimates and inflicted enormous material losses on a majority of Armenians.

In response to the crisis in the Ottoman Empire, a new political group called the Young Turks seized power by revolution in 1908. From the Young Turks, the Committee of Union and Progress (CUP), *Ittihad ve Terakki Jemiyeti*, emerged at the head of the government in a coup staged in 1913. It was led by a triumvirate: Enver, Minister of War; Talaat, Minister of the Interior (Grand Vizier in 1917); and Jemal, Minister of the Marine. The CUP espoused an ultranationalistic ideology which advocated the formation of an exclusively Turkish state. It also subscribed to an ideology of aggrandizement through conquest directed eastward toward other regions inhabited by Turkic peoples, at that time subject to the Russian Empire. The CUP also steered Istanbul toward closer diplomatic and military relations with Imperial Germany. When World War I broke out in August 1914, the Ottoman Empire formed part of the Triple Alliance with the other Central Powers, Germany and Austria-Hungary, and it declared war on Russia and its Western allies, Great Britain and France.

The Deportations Begin

The Ottoman armies initially suffered a string of defeats which they made up for with a series of easy military victories in the Caucasus in 1918 before the Central Powers capitulated later that same year. Whether retreating or advancing, the Ottoman army used the occasion of war to wage a collateral campaign of massacre against the civilian Armenian population in the regions in which warfare was being conducted. These measures were part of the genocidal program secretly adopted by the CUP and implemented under the cover of war. They coincided with the CUP's larger program to eradicate the Armenians from Turkey and neighboring countries for the purpose of creating a new Pan-Turanian empire. Through the spring and summer of 1915, in all areas outside the war zones, the Armenian population was ordered deported from their homes.

Convoys consisting of tens of thousands including men, women, and children were driven hundreds of miles toward the Syrian desert.

The deportations were disguised as a resettlement program. The brutal treatment of the deportees, most of whom were made to walk to their destinations, made it apparent that the deportations were mainly intended as death marches. Moreover, the policy of deportation surgically removed the Armenians from the rest of society and disposed of great masses of people with little or no destruction of property. The displacement process, therefore, also served as a major opportunity orchestrated by the CUP for the plundering of the material wealth of the Armenians and proved an effortless method of expropriating all of their immovable properties.

Mass Killings and Starvation

The genocidal intent of the CUP measures was also evidenced by the mass killings that accompanied the deportations. Earlier, Armenian soldiers in the Ottoman forces had been disarmed and either worked to death in labor battalions or outright executed in small batches. With the elimination of the able-bodied men from the Armenian population, the deportations proceeded with little resistance. The convoys were frequently attacked by bands of killers specifically organized for the purpose of slaughtering the Armenians. As its instrument of extermination, the government had authorized the formation of gangs of butchers—mostly convicts released from prison expressly enlisted in the units of the so-called Special Organization, *Teshkilâti Mahsusa*. This secret outfit was headed by the most ferocious partisans of the CUP who took it upon themselves to carry out the orders of the central government with the covert instructions of their party leaders. A sizable portion of the deportees, including women and children, were indiscriminately killed in massacres along the deportation routes. The cruelty characterizing the killing process was heightened by the fact that it was frequently carried out by the sword in terrifying episodes of bloodshed. Furthermore, for the survivors, their witnessing of the murder of friends and relatives with the mass of innocent persons was the source of serious trauma. Many younger women and some orphaned children were also abducted and placed in bondage in Turkish and Muslim homes resulting in another type of trauma characterized by the shock of losing both family and one's sense of identity. These women and children were frequently forbidden to grieve, were employed as unpaid laborers, and were required to assimilate the language and religion of their captors.

The government had made no provisions for the feeding of the deported population. Starvation took an enormous toll much as exhaustion felled the elderly, the weaker and the infirm. Deportees were denied food and water in a deliberate effort to hasten death. The survivors who reached northern Syria were collected at a number of concentration camps whence they were sent further south to die under the scorching sun of the desert. Through methodically organized deportation, systematic massacre, deliberate starvation and dehydration, and continuous brutalization, the Ottoman government reduced its Armenian population to a frightened mass of famished individuals whose families and communities had been destroyed in a single stroke.

Resistance to the deportations was infrequent. Only in one instance did the entire population of an Armenian settlement manage to evade death. The mountaineers of Musa Dagh defended themselves in the heights above their villages until French naval vessels in the eastern Mediterranean detected them and transported them to safety. The inhabitants of the city of Van in eastern Armenia defended themselves until relieved by advancing Russian forces. They abandoned the city in May 1915, a month after the siege was lifted, when the Russian Army withdrew. The fleeing population was hunted down mercilessly by Turkish irregular forces. Inland towns that resisted, such as Urfa (Edessa), were reduced to rubble by artillery. The survival of the Armenians in large part is credited not to acts of resistance, but to the humanitarian intervention led by American Ambassador Henry Morgenthau. Although the Allied Powers expressly warned the Ottoman government about its policy of genocide, ultimately it was through Morgenthau's efforts that the plight of the Armenians was publicized in the United States. The U.S. Congress authorized the formation of a relief committee which raised funds to feed "the starving Armenians." Near East Relief, as the committee was eventually known, saved tens of thousands of lives. After the war, it headed a large-scale effort to rehabilitate the survivors who were mostly left to their own devices in their places of deportation. By setting up refugee camps, orphanages, medical clinics and educational facilities, Near East Relief rescued the surviving Armenian population.

On Trial for War Crimes

In the post-war period nearly four hundred of the key CUP officials implicated in the atrocities committed against the Armenians were arrested. A number of domestic military tribunals were convened which brought charges ranging from the unconstitutional seizure of power and subversion of the legal government, the conduct of a war of aggression, and conspiring the liquidation of the Armenian population, to more explicit capital crimes, including massacre. Some of the accused were found guilty of the charges. Most significantly, the ruling triumvirate was condemned to death. They, however, eluded justice by fleeing abroad. Their escape left the matter of avenging the countless victims to a clandestine group of survivors that tracked down the CUP arch conspirators. Talaat, the principal architect of the Armenian genocide, was killed in 1921 in Berlin where he had gone into hiding. His assassin was arrested and tried in a German court which acquitted him.

Most of those implicated in war crimes evaded justice and many joined the new Nationalist Turkish movement led by Mustafa Kemal. In a series of military campaigns against Russian Armenia in 1920, against the refugee Armenians who had returned to Cilicia in southern Turkey in 1921, and against the Greek army that had occupied Izmir (Smyrna) where the last intact Armenian community in Anatolia still existed in 1922, the Nationalist forces completed the process of eradicating the Armenians through further expulsions and massacres. When Turkey was declared a republic in 1923 and received international recognition, the Armenian Question and all related matters of resettlement and restitution were swept aside and soon forgotten.

In all, it is estimated that up to a million and a half Armenians perished at the hands of Ottoman and Turkish military and paramilitary forces and through atrocities intentionally inflicted to eliminate the Armenian demographic presence in Turkey. In the process, the population of historic Armenia at the eastern extremity of Anatolia was wiped off the map. With their disappearance, an ancient people which had inhabited the Armenian highlands for three thousand years lost its historic homeland and was forced into exile and a new diaspora. The surviving refugees spread around the world and eventually settled in some two dozen countries on all continents of the globe. Triumphant in its total annihilation of the Armenians and relieved of any obligations to the victims and survivors, the Turkish Republic adopted a policy of dismissing the charge of genocide and denying that the deportations and atrocities had constituted part of a deliberate plan to exterminate the Armenians. When the Red Army sovietized what remained of Russian Armenia in 1920, the Armenians had been compressed into an area amounting to no more than ten percent of the territories of their historic homeland. Armenians annually commemorate the Genocide on April 24 at the site of memorials raised by the survivors in all their communities around the world.

Stalin's Government Created the Ukrainian Famine-Genocide

Askold Krushelnycky

Askold Krushelnycky is a London-born journalist whose parents fled Ukraine during World War II. He is a foreign correspondent for several newspapers, including the Chicago Tribune, *and he has recently authored* An Orange Revolution: A Personal Journey Through Ukrainian History. *In the following viewpoint he asserts that the 1932–1933 Ukrainian famine was created by Soviet leader Joseph Stalin. Fearing that some farmers had become too self-reliant, Stalin and his Communist regime created a class conflict between the wealthier peasants (kulaks) and the poorer ones, which destabilized the region and led to the death and displacement of millions of Ukrainians.*

[The year 2003] marks the 70th anniversary of a collectivization program masterminded by former Soviet leader Josef Stalin that claimed the lives of millions of people, mostly Ukrainian peasant farmers.

An artificial famine of devastating proportions was the culmination of a savage piece of human engineering designed to eliminate an economic class that the Communists viewed as their fierce opponents. It was also intended to break the will of Ukrainians—Communists and non-Communists alike—who clung to their national identity.

The tsarist-era owners [those who owned farms when Russia was governed by the tsars (or czars)] of sweeping plots of land had already been killed or driven out by the 1917 Communist revolution. But the Soviet leadership also despised

Askold Krushelnycky, "Ukraine Famine," FamineGenocide.com, 2003. Copyright © 2003 RFE/RL, Inc. Reprinted with the permission of Radio Free Europe/Radio Liberty, 1201 Connecticut Ave. N.W., Washington, DC 20036. www.rferl.org.

the millions of peasant farmers who took their place, maintaining small farms and growing mostly grain. To the Communists, such farmers were a threatening example of self-reliance and capitalism.

Stalin, in particular, saw Ukrainian peasants as forming the front line of the Ukrainian nationalist movement he so intensely disliked. He resented the compromises Moscow had been forced to make with Ukrainian Communists—compromises that gave them a degree of autonomy and that saw a revival of Ukrainian culture and language.

"Dekulakization"

The Soviets divided the peasants into different categories. The primary class enemy was the kulak, relatively well-off farmers who could afford to own several heads of livestock and occasionally hire help with plowing or harvesting. To eliminate the kulaks, the Communists hoped to gain the support from poorer peasant farmers by drumming up class resentment.

In late 1929, Stalin launched a "dekulakization" program centered on Ukraine but encompassing the North Caucasus—which had high proportions of ethnic Ukrainians among peoples like the Kuban Cossacks—and Kazakhstan.

A venomous propaganda war fomented hatred against kulaks and their families, portraying them as a threat equal to an invading foreign army. Communists and brigades of so-called "activists" backed by Soviet secret police brutally stripped the kulaks of their homes and possessions, shooting those who resisted and deporting millions to Siberia and the Far North. . . .

Around 7.5 million people, including one million in Kazakhstan, are estimated to have died during the period of "dekulakization." Many kulaks resorted to slaughtering their livestock and burning down their homes rather than seeing them confiscated. Thousands were shot for opposing the brigades sent to strip them of their property. Many died during the weeks of transport in unheated trains to labor camps, with little food to sustain them. The largest percentage perished in the first years after their deportation. . . .

The Beginning of Collectivization

Together with "dekulakization," a process of collectivization was under way. The Communists imposed crippling grain demands on peasant farmers to make it unprofitable to sustain their small holdings and pressure them into joining collective farms.

Moscow sent 25,000 trusted Communists from Russia to organize collective and state farms. The secret police and often the army were used to terrorize peasants into joining. The Communists were dismayed that even after the vicious propaganda campaign most peasants sympathized more with kulaks than with the Communist Party.

Many of these poorer peasants were ultimately reclassified as kulaks themselves. Most joined the collective farms reluctantly. Many were executed for trying to sell off or slaughter their livestock rather than donating them to the collective farms.

The authorities worked vigorously to extract the unrealistically high grain yields demanded by Moscow, leaving pitifully little with which the farmers could feed themselves and their families.

The collective farms were notoriously inefficient. Even so—and against the pleas of even senior Ukrainian Communist leaders—Stalin in 1932 increased grain quotas in Ukraine, the North Caucasus, and Russia's Volga [River] region. The demand made famine inevitable.

Communist loyalists during the Soviet era—and some even today—have blamed the famine on a poor harvest in 1932. But even Soviet records show the year's harvest as satisfactory. . . .

As hunger begun to take a firmer grip on the peasant population, the Communist authorities used force and terror to fulfill the grain quotas, which left peasants and collective farms with little or nothing to sustain themselves with. Thousands of peasants who tried to hide grain or other food to feed their families were executed, as were many local Communist officials who objected to a policy that brought starvation to many areas as 1932 approached its end.

The book *Harvest of Sorrow* by British historian Robert Conquest is considered the most comprehensive study of the period. In it, he says Stalin was aware that the excessive grain requisitions would lead to famine, but persisted in order to destroy what he saw as the double threat of peasant anti-Communism and Ukrainian nationalism. . . .

Impossibly High Grain Quotas

Oleksa Sonipul was 10 in 1933 and lived in a village in northern Ukraine. She said by the beginning of that year, famine was so widespread people had been reduced to eating grass, tree bark, roots, berries, frogs, birds, and even earthworms.

Desperate hunger drove people to sell off all of their possessions for any food they could find. At night, an eerie silence fell over the village, where all the livestock and chickens had long since been killed for food and exhausted villagers went to bed early.

But Communist requisition brigades looking to fulfill the impossibly high grain quotas continued to search even those villages where inhabitants were already dying from starvation. They used metal poles to probe the ground and potential hiding places where they suspected grain could be hidden.

Some of the brigade members, fueled by Soviet hate campaigns against the peasants, acted without mercy, taking away the last crumbs of food from starving families knowing they were condemning even small children to death. Any peasant who resisted was shot. Rape and robbery also took place. . . .

Massive Starvation

As food ran out in the villages, thousands of desperate people trekked to beg for food in towns and cities. Food was available in cities, although strictly controlled through ration coupons. But residents were forbidden to help the starving peasants and doctors were not allowed to aid the skeletal villagers, who were left to die on the streets. . . .

Grain and potatoes continued to be harvested in Ukraine, driven by the demand of Stalin's quotas. But the inefficiency of the Soviet transportation system meant that tons of food literally rotted uneaten—sometimes in the open and within the view of those dying of starvation. . . .

In the countryside, entire villages were being wiped out. The hunger drove many people to desperation and madness. Many instances of cannibalism were recorded, with people living off the remains of other starvation victims or in some instances resorting to murder. Most peasant families had five or six children, and some mothers killed their weakest children in order to feed the others. . . .

Mykhaylo Naumenko was 11 years old in 1933. His father was executed for refusing to join a nearby collective farm. Mykhaylo was left with his mother and siblings to face the famine without a provider. He said people were shot for trying to steal grain or potatoes from the local collective farm, which was surrounded by barbed wire and guarded by armed men. He said people were executed even for trying to pick up a few loose seeds dropped on the ground.

"A tragedy developed. People became swollen, they died by the tens each day. The collective farm authorities appointed six men to collect and bury the dead. From our village of 75 homes, by May, 24 houses were empty where all the inhabitants had died."

Naumenko also witnessed instances of cannibalism. He said he first discovered that his neighbors were eating human flesh after one of them, called Tetyana, refused to share her meat with him despite the fact he had just helped bury her father.

"I saw Tetyana eating chicken meat and saw there was a lot of it. I approached her and asked her for some, but she refused to give me any. Because it was human flesh."

Hundreds were executed or killed by other villagers for cannibalism. Soviet records show that around 1,000 people were still serving sentences for cannibalism in prison camps on the White Sea at the end of the 1930s.

Olena Mukniak was 10 in 1933 and lived in a village in the Poltavschyna region with her mother, older sister, and younger brother. Her father had left for the Donbas area in search of food. In the village, Mukniak said people picked through horse manure to find grain, stewed leather boots, and toasted leaves and tree bark.

"What do you do if there's nothing to eat? We collected birch leaves and toasted them and ate them. What else could we do?"

Her sister worked at the collective farm and received a small piece of bread every day for all four of them. But it was not enough to keep them all alive.

"My brother died from starvation. He was small and there was nothing to eat. What could our mother give us to eat when there was nothing? My sister brought us a little piece of bread once a day and we gulped it down and waited until the next day. But you wanted food all the time. My brother was younger than I and he died because he needed to eat. And our mother could give nothing."

Many people met their deaths with quiet resignation, praying and comforting their starving children with fairy tales.

Suffering in Silence

Not all authorities were untouched by the tragedy. Some of the Communist activists and officials supervising the grain expropriation were horrified at what they saw and protested to their superiors or tried to provide food for the starving villagers. For their efforts, they were executed.

For scores of senior Ukrainian Communists, the famine and Stalin's attack on the Ukrainian cultural revival were cause for their final disillusionment with the ideology they had served. Many of them committed suicide rather than face torture and show trials.

Until the fall of communism, most of the villager eyewitnesses who survived the famine were wary of telling their stories. Even now, many are reluctant to talk about that period because they see many Soviet-era holdovers still in positions of power.

The memories that seem to haunt them most are those of watching their loved ones die. Teodora Soroka, who lost nearly every member of her family to "dekulakization" and famine, says such memories can never be erased. Nor does she want to forget them.

"My little sister died of hunger in my arms. She was begging for a piece of bread, because to have a piece of bread in the house meant life. She pleaded for me to give her a bit of bread. I was crying and told her that we didn't have any. She told me that I wanted her to die. Believe me, it's painful even now. I was little myself then. I cried, but my heart was not torn to shreds because I couldn't understand why this was all happening. But today, and ever since I became an adult, I haven't spent a day in my life when I haven't cried. I have never gone to sleep without thinking about what happened to my family." . . .

World Remains Unaware of Tragedy

Estimates of how many people died in Stalin's engineered famine of 1933 vary. But they are staggering in their scale—between seven and 11 million people.

But despite the horrific number of people who died, the world is relatively unfamiliar with this grisly chapter in Soviet history which claimed lives on the same scale as the [Nazi] holocaust. One of the main reasons is that the Germans were eventually defeated, and thousands of eyewitnesses told their stories about concentration camps and massacres. The experience was also captured unforgettably in photographs, film, and written accounts, and many of those responsible for the genocide were captured and put on trial.

Lyubomyr Luciuk is the director of research at the Ukrainian Canadian Civil Liberties Association. He explained why there was no such opportunity to investigate the famine in the Soviet Union.

"The Nazis were so completely and utterly defeated and had no apologists other than a few nuts after the second world war. The Soviet Union, in contrast, imploded," Luciuk said. "There was no military conquest. Ideologically, perhaps, it was defeated. But in a sense, the regime of yesteryear—many of its functionaries, administrators, and bureaucrats—simply changed their shirts and became nationalists or patriots overnight. The archival record is still not entirely available. There has been no Nuremberg trial, if you like, to bring the many thousands, if not hundreds of thousands of people who served the Soviet regime to justice."

British historian Robert Conquest is an expert on the period and his 1986 study of the famine, *Harvest of Sorrow* brought much information about the tragedy to Western audiences for the first time. Conquest said another contrast between the famine and the holocaust is that while Adolf Hitler had written down much of what he intended to do, Stalin did not go on record about the famine. . . .

But Conquest said more evidence has emerged since the disintegration of the USSR allowed greater access to Soviet archives. He says he himself has uncovered documented evidence that shows Stalin knew that hundreds of thousands of peasants were trying to enter Russia in search of food. . . .

Conquest is in no doubt that the famine was primarily aimed at Ukrainians and that Stalin hated not only the country peasants but even senior Communist leaders, like Mykola Skrypnyk, who eventually killed himself. . . .

Walter Duranty's Coverup

Luciuk of the Ukrainian Canadian Civil Liberties Association has a different theory for why news of the famine never reached the West. He blamed a number of Western journalists based in Moscow at the time who knew of the forced starvation but chose not to write about it or deliberately covered it up.

The journalist he says played the most influential role in the cover-up was the *New York Times* correspondent Walter Duranty. A drug addict with a shady reputation, Duranty was also an avid fan of Stalin, whom he described as "the world's greatest living statesman." He was granted the first American interview with the Soviet leader and received privileged information from the secretive regime.

Duranty confided to a British diplomat at the time that he thought 10 million people had perished in the famine. But when other journalists who had traveled to Ukraine began writing about the horrific famine raging there, Duranty branded their information as anti-Soviet lies. Conquest believes that Duranty was being blackmailed by the Soviet secret police over his sexual activities, which reportedly included bisexuality and necrophilia. . . .

Duranty died in 1957 an impoverished drunk. Luciuk said that when details about the famine finally came into the open, Duranty was credited with coining the famously callous phrase, "You can't make an omelet without breaking eggs."

Luciuk said he hopes Ukraine, meanwhile, will do more to educate its own population about the famine. Since gaining independence, successive Ukrainian governments have done little to publicize the episode for fear of instigating a controversy with the country's still-powerful Communist Party, which continues to deny the famine was deliberately organized. Moreover, many of those who took part in the executions, deportations, and confiscation of food are still alive and receiving state pensions.

In February [2003], the Ukrainian parliament conducted a special hearing about the famine. The deputy prime minister for humanitarian issues, Dmytro Tabachnuk, said the famine was a deliberate terrorist act that claimed the lives of up to 10 million people. He said the government is planning to build a National Famine Memorial Complex.

CHAPTER 3

The Prevention
of Genocide

The Right to Bear Arms Can Prevent Future Genocides

Dave Kopel

In the following viewpoint Dave Kopel, former assistant attorney general of the State of Colorado and contributing editor to the Michigan Law Review, argues that the right to bear arms is essential in the prevention of genocide. He asserts that national gun ownership restrictions led to the genocide in Darfur, Sudan, by leaving citizens defenseless against rebel groups and the government. Kopel also notes that the current gun-control legislation being advanced by the United Nations will contribute to the development of future genocides.

The international gun prohibition lobbies and their United Nations allies insist that there is no personal right of self-defense—that people should be forced to rely exclusively on the government [for] protection. The prohibitionists also insist that there is no human right for people to possess the means of self-defense, such as firearms. But what are people supposed to do when the government itself starts killing people? The genocide in Darfur, Sudan, is the direct result of the types of gun laws which the United Nations is trying to impose all over the world. Millions of people have already died because of such laws, and millions more will die unless the U.N. is stopped. Like Iran today and Afghanistan under the Taliban, Sudan is ruled by a totalitarian, Islamist Arab government. The current regime took power in a military coup in 1989, and immediately began imposing Islamic law throughout the country, and perpetrating genocide. The genocide targets have varied: people in the central highlands were the first victims. Then the black Africans of south Sudan, who

Dave Kopel, "Gun Bans and Genocide: The Disarming Facts," America's First Freedom/ www.davekopel.com, August 2006. www.davekopel.com/2A/Foreign/gun-bans-and-genocide.htm. Reproduced by permission.

are mainly Christians or Animists. The most recent genocide victims are the people of Darfur, a Texas-sized region in western Sudan.

The Darfuris are Muslims, but like the majority of Sudan's population, they are black Africans, in contrast to the Arabs who control the government.

The foundation of Sudan's genocide is, as with almost every other genocide in world history, the disarmament of the victims.

Sudan's Gun-Control Statutes

In Sudan, it is virtually impossible for an average citizen to lawfully acquire and possess the means for self-defense. According to the national gun-control statutes, a gun licensee must be over 30 years of age, must have a specified social and economic status, and must be examined physically by a doctor. Females have even more difficulty meeting these requirements because of social and occupational limitations.

When these restrictions are finally overcome, there are additional restrictions on the amount of ammunition one may possess, making it nearly impossible for a law-abiding gun owner to achieve proficiency with firearms. A handgun owner, for example, can only purchase 15 rounds of ammunition a year. The penalties for violation of Sudan's firearms laws are severe, and can include capital punishment.

Consequences of Gun Laws

The practical application of the gun laws is different. If you are someone the government wants to slaughter—such as all the black Africans of southern and western Sudan, regardless of their religion—then you are absolutely forbidden to possess a firearm. A U.S. Department of State document notes: "After President Bashir seized power in 1989, the new government disarmed non-Arab ethnic groups but allowed politically loyal Arab allies to keep their weapons."

On the other hand, if you're an Arab who wants to kill blacks, then Sudan's gun control laws became awfully loose. In Darfur, there has been a long rivalry between camel-riding Arab nomads and black African pastoralists. The Arabs consider the blacks to be racially inferior, and fit only for slavery. In *Darfur Rising*, the International Crisis Group explains: "Beginning in the mid-1980s, successive governments in Khartoum inflamed matters by supporting and arming the Arab tribes, in part to prevent the southern rebels from gaining a foothold in the region. . . . Arabs formed militias, burned African villages, and killed thousands. Africans in turn formed self-defense groups, members of which eventually became the first Darfur insurgents to appear in 2003." . . .

Likewise, Peter Verney, of the London-based *Sudan Update*, writes that the government armed the Arabs "while removing the weapons of the farmers, the Fur, Masalit and Zaghawa." . . .

While the blacks are forbidden to possess arms, the Arabs are given arms by the government—five or six guns per person according to Amnesty International. The Arabs are then formed into terrorist gangs known as Janjaweed (literally, "evil men on horseback" or "devil on a horse").

Armed Rebel Groups

In both south Sudan (Christian and Animist Africans) and western Sudan (that is, Darfur, inhabited by Muslim Africans) there were armed rebel groups. That these resistance groups had been able to acquire weapons illegally was a great affront to the United Nations and the gun prohibition lobbies, who denounce any form of gun possession by "non-state actors." A "non-state actor" is any person or group whose arms possession is not approved by the government; examples include the Sudanese who were fighting the genocidal dictatorship in their country, the Jews in the Warsaw ghetto, and the American revolutionaries.

The Sudanese resistance movements, although able to acquire some arms for their own operations, did not have the resources to protect the many isolated villages in the vast nation.

So with the black villagers disarmed—thanks to Sudan's strict gun laws—and the Arab gangs well-armed (thanks to the government), the stage was set for genocide. Typically, the mounted Arab gangs would attack a village on the ground, while the Sudanese military provided air support and bombed the village.

In the south Sudan, the genocide program killed 2.2 million victims, and drove 4.5 million from their homes....

Darfur Was the Next Target

[In Darfur], the Janjaweed have caused the deaths of up to 400,000 black Sudanese, have raped many thousands, and have forced over 2 million black Sudanese into refugee camps....

Notably, the majority of villages bombed were villages where there were no armed rebels. Thus, the destruction of the villages should be seen not as an overzealous form of counter-insurgency warfare, but rather as a deliberate attempt to destroy an entire society. The ethnic cleansing of Darfur has been so thorough that, literally, there are no villages left to burn.

The victim villagers are generally unarmed. Amnesty International reported the testimony of a villager who complained: "None of us had arms and we were not able to resist the attack." One underarmed villager lamented: "I tried to take my spear to protect my family, but they threatened me with a gun, so I stopped. The six Arabs then raped my daughter in front of me, my wife and my other children."

In cases when the villagers were able to resist, the cost to the marauders rose: Human Rights Watch reported that "some of Kudun's residents mobilized to protect themselves, and fifteen of the attackers were reportedly killed."

The Pittsburgh *Tribune-Review* asked a U.S. State Department official why there were no reports of the Darfur victims fighting back. "Some do defend themselves," he explained. But he added that the perpetrators have helicopters and automatic rifles, whereas the victims have only machetes. . . .

U.N. Inaction and Protocols

The United Nations has done nothing meaningful to stop the genocide in Sudan. An African Union [AU] "peacekeeping" force was dispatched, but that small and low-quality force was only assigned to protecting international aid workers at refugee camps. The AU is not supposed to protect the actual victims. . . .

Because the international community has utterly failed to protect the Darfuris, they have every moral right to protect themselves. In an article in the *Notre Dame Law Review*, Paul Gallant, Joanne Eisen, and I argue that the Genocide Convention gives the Darfuris a formal legal right to [bear] arms.

A teenage girl with a gun might not be the ideal soldier. But she is certainly not the ideal rape victim. It is not particularly difficult to learn how to use a firearm to shoot a would-be rapist from a distance of fifteen or twenty-five feet away. Would every one of the Janjaweed Arab bullies who enjoy raping African girls be brave enough to dare trying to rape a girl who was carrying a rifle or a handgun?

The United Nations, however, is hard at work to make sure that genocide victims in Sudan, and anywhere else in Africa, will not be able to resist.

Sudan is covered by a U.N.–backed treaty called the "The Nairobi Protocol for the Prevention, Control and Reduction of Small Arms and Light Weapons in the Great Lakes Region and the Horn of Africa." The protocol was signed in 2004 by representatives of Burundi, Democratic Republic of the Congo, Djibouti, Eritrea, Ethiopia, Kenya, Rwanda, Seychelles, Sudan, Uganda, and Tanzania.

The [protocol] requires universal gun registration, complete provision of all civilian-owned semi-automatic rifles, "heavy minimum sentences for ... the carrying of unlicensed small arms," as well as programs to encourage citizens to surrender their guns, widespread searches for firearms, educational programs to discourage gun ownership, and other policies to disarm the public.

The U.N. is, successfully, pushing for gun control in East African nations with *current* genocides: Sudan, Democratic Republic of the Congo, and Ethiopia. Several others, such as Rwanda and Uganda, have recent histories of genocide against disarmed victims. Quite plainly, the U.N. believes that resisting an actual genocide in progress is not a sufficient reason for someone to want to own a gun. . . .

The prohibition lobbies and their U.N. allies will tell you that people never need guns for protection—not for protection from rapists, and not for protection from genocidaires. Governments and the United Nations will protect everyone. The tragedy of disarmed victims in the Sudan, and all over Africa, shows the deadly falseness of the prohibitionist promise. For decades, millions of Africans have been slaughtered by genocidal tyrants while the rest of the world stood idle. Now, the United Nations has become objectively complicit in genocide, by trying to ensure that never again will anyone targeted for genocide be able to use a firearm to save herself or her family.

The Right to Bear Arms Cannot Prevent Future Genocides

Daniel Nexon

In the following viewpoint Daniel Nexon, professor of government at Georgetown University, argues that allowing private citizens to own guns is not a useful means for preventing future genocides. By examining past examples of genocides and mass violence, he determines that there are more risks than benefits to encouraging gun ownership, including the potential for government leaders to view gun-owning minorities as a threat to national security. Ultimately, he concludes that the only way of resisting a tyrannical government is to train and equip an insurgency.

After the 1989 massacre of pro-democracy advocates in Tiananmen Square [in China] by the People's Liberation Army, the NRA [National Rifle Association] ran advertisements claiming that if the protesters had been armed, they could've defended themselves and thus prevented the anti-democracy crackdown. This kind of argument, rooted in the (correct) conviction that the ultimate recourse against tyranny is armed insurrection, has a long history both in political theory and in gun-rights advocacy.

Adopting this logic, Joe Katzman, of [the blog] *Winds of Change*, writes that the world's indifference to the mass violence in Zimbabwe has convinced him that gun ownership is a basic right. . . .

My gut response is: provocative idea, but no cigar. . . .

Daniel Nexon, "Guns and Genocide," *The Duck of Minerva*, June 11, 2005. http://duckofminerva.blogspot.com/2005_06_01_duckofminerva_archive.html. Reproduced by permission of Professor Daniel H. Nexon.

Subpopulations and Genocide

A subpopulation is vulnerable to genocide if they are, in some significant respects, weaker than the groups who seek to eliminate them. Having state-of-the-art personal weaponry can help matters, but not if the subpopulation is dispersed, significantly outnumbered, or otherwise at the "short end" of a power asymmetry. In this respect, claims that "the right to bear arms is the only reliable way to prevent genocide" should really be understood as "in a world in which all subpopulations were secure against attack, there would be no genocide." This is certainly true, but trivially so.

Security Dilemmas

Security, of course, is often relative. The greater the capabilities of one side, the less secure the other side. This is [writer] Bill Wallo's point:

> But the presence of a weapon doesn't always breed safety—sometimes it breeds an arms race because then everyone is caught in a Prisoner's Dilemma of deciding what to carry. The guy with a knife has an advantage over the guy without one, and the guy with a gun has an advantage over both—so why not pack a gun? This sort of escalation in ostensible "defense" can have tragic results—hence the viability of societal restrictions that basically require the scaling back of the arms race between citizens.

The problem here is actually a Security Dilemma. The Security Dilemma is related to the Prisoner's Dilemma, in that both are cases in which rational choices produce Pareto-inefficient outcomes [a decision that will make at least one individual better off without making the situations for others worse]. But unlike in the Prisoner's Dilemma, the problem Bill points to is one of signaling: if a subpopulation acquires a boatload of weapons to defend itself against possible genocide, it may signal to the majority population that it *really* does have aggressive intentions against them; thus the subpopulation may "prove" that the only way to deal with it is to ethnically cleanse or exterminate it.

In fact, many instances of mass violence and genocide do involve situations when a subpopulation seeks to arm itself in order to gain political autonomy (e.g., the Bosnian Muslims, the Kurds), or when states perceive the presence of the subpopulation as a threat to national integrity and state security (e.g., the Armenians). Thus, regardless of whether or not arms procurement by a minority group is purely defensive in character, political leaders have a lot of reasons to see that activity as a justification for initiating genocide.

Genocide and Mass Violence

Such perverse effects are particularly important once we recognize that *genocide is a subset of mass violence.*

Genocide can be extremely deadly (e.g., six million Jews, around twice as many "Kulaks" [Russian peasants]) but nongenocidal mass violence kills a lot of people. . . . The deaths in the Congo, however, are the consequence of a society awash in guns and warlords (thanks to factors ranging from the lucrative diamond trade to external support for rebel forces), as well as a state that no longer maintains control over violence in its territory.

Moreover, ethnic violence kills most of its victims indirectly rather than directly. The most deadly effects of such intergroup conflicts tend to stem from the displacement of people from their homes; i.e., from the secondary impact of disease, poverty, and starvation. So let's say, for the sake of argument, that we could stop genocide by creating a world of mutually hostile subgroups armed to the teeth. Such a world would almost certainly involve a lot of intergroup violence that, in the end, would probably cost more lives than the alternative.

Democracy and Genocide

It is true that states disarm minorities as part of the process leading to genocide. The Turks began the Armenian genocide, for example, by confiscating Armenian weapons. But here I'm reminded of [Oxford University history professor] Michael Mann's quip about [University of Hawaii political science professor] R.J. Rummel's genocide argument. Rummel argues that democracy is the best check against mass killing, because democracies do not kill their own citizens. Mann counters that democracies do kill their own citizens, it's just that by the time they're actually slaughtering subpopulations they don't look particularly democratic anymore. Saying that the right to bear arms prevents genocide is no different than saying that due process, equal protection, or freedom of association prevent genocide. If we could guarantee those rights everywhere in the world, there wouldn't be any genocide. If we can't guarantee them—which we can't—then we also can't guarantee a right to bear arms.

The State and Security

Ultimately, what all this comes down to is a tragic irony of politics. The modern state's "monopoly on the legitimate use of force" has created historically unequalled security for many of the world's people. Given the choice, even libertarians would probably admit that living in such "statist" societies as the US, Canada, or France is a far more attractive choice than living in the anarchy of the present-day Congo, Somalia in the early 1990s, or any other "failed state." But it is precisely what makes the state the most effective guarantor of security and prosperity humanity has yet devised—its enormously effective control over organized violence—that also makes it capable of killing and slaughtering on an unprecedented scale.

Train and Equip Insurgency

Regardless, simply throwing guns at the Zimbabwean political opposition is probably not a good idea, as they would be crushed by the better-trained and better-organized govern-ment forces. If we want a policy to overthrow the government, then we should expect to train and equip an insurgency, i.e., engage in some form of intervention.

The International Criminal Court Will Prevent Future Genocides

Peter Barcroft and David Donat Cattin .

Peter Barcroft, Senior Programme Officer, and David Donat Cattin, Legal Advisor, work for the Parliamentarians for Global Action (PGA), a nonprofit, nonpartisan network of elected legislators with members in more than one hundred countries around the globe, which aims to promote democracy and human rights. In the following viewpoint they argue that while it is too early to accurately assess whether the International Criminal Court, established in 2002, will deter future genocides, early indications have shown considerable promise in the court's potential for enacting global justice.

In a world where a premium is justifiably placed on hard facts or evidence/indicators of hard facts, measuring the deterrent effect of an institution such as the International Criminal Court (ICC) will always present something of a challenge. There is no readily available mechanism pursuant to which we can accurately assess the Court's 'long arm' or 'long term' preventative effect. Instead, we could be faced with a more vague 'no news is good news/silence is golden' scenario. Because of the many variables often present, deterrence, as a general proposition, is inherently difficult to gauge. Nevertheless, it has been proven that well-educated would-be criminals are often deterred by the certainty or high probability of punishment, which makes their criminal plan too risky and not "cost-effective" enough: this is particularly true for would-be

Peter Barcroft and David Donat Cattin, "A Deterrent International Criminal Court—The Ultimate Objective," PGA International Law and Human Rights Programme, for the III Session for the Consultative Assembly of Parliamentarians for the ICC and the Rule of Law, Parliament of New Zealand (Wellington), December 6–7, 2004. iccnow.org/ documents/WellingtonPGAPaperonICCDeterrence7Dec04.pdf. Reproduced by permission of Parliamentarians for Global Action.

perpetrators of "white-collar crimes" and corruption. The area of international crimes still needs to be tested by statistical analysis, but the fact that the ICC Prosecutor's strategy is focusing on the "persons bearing the greatest responsibility for the most serious atrocities" (e.g., political and military leaders) may lead to an assessment of the ICC impact on the future commission of these crimes in a similar vein in which effective national jurisdictions help deter white-collar crimes.

Potential for Deterrence

A number of unique factors arise for consideration insofar as the potential preventive effect of the ICC may be concerned:

- The ICC is still at an embryonic stage in its existence. It is yet to complete its first case. It must be afforded an opportunity to establish its credentials. This, by its very nature, is not an overnight process, but may take a number of years.

- Does the establishment *alone* of the ICC have a deterrent effect? Its permanent status, in contrast to the *ad hoc* [for a single purpose] nature of the tribunals for the former Yugoslavia, Rwanda and Sierra Leone, undoubtedly sends a strong signal *per se* [by itself]. It is here to stay. At the same time, however, the real strength of its deterrent force, at least to some extent, may have to be 'earned' through the effective and impartial conduct of cases during the course of the coming years. Even a relatively small number of well-managed cases should serve to consolidate the reputation of the Court and, consequently, instill more hesitancy in the minds of potential future perpetrators of the crimes set out in the Rome Statute [the nickname for the United Nations Diplomatic Conference of Plenipotentiaries on Establishment of an International Criminal Court]. By its deeds, the ICC has an opportunity to emit an unambiguous message that it is an institution which 'means business', that it will act decisively, where there is an unwillingness or inability to do so on the part of national authorities. Action will undoubtedly speak louder than words to those who in the future may contemplate commission of any of the heinous crimes set out in the Rome Statute.

- Even if not completely conclusive, an increase in the number of national prosecutions in the next 5–10 years of individuals charged with genocide, crimes against humanity or war crimes, could also be reasonably credited to a beneficial, knock-on 'contagion' effect of the ICC's presence in The Hague [the Netherlands' governmental center, and home to the UN's International Court of Justice]. As a corollary, although perhaps more optimistically, were there to be an appreciable decline in the commission of the crimes set out in the Rome Statute in the coming years, it would not be unreasonable to attribute this to the 'long shadow' of the ICC. After all, this would be the ultimate and ideal indicator of success in the fight against impunity. The initial practise of the ICC can [be] analysed in this perspective, especially with respect to the developing situation of Northern Uganda, as outlined below.

- It ought to be emphasised that *whether or not the ICC will in time wield a significant deterrent effect will not, and cannot, depend exclusively on its conduct alone.* States must actively discharge their responsibilities under national law and prosecute individuals charged with the crimes in question, emboldened in this task by the very existence of the ICC. Parliamentarians, *as legislators*, have a key role to play to equip their national systems with the effective laws and remedies to fight impunity and complement the action of the ICC. The

ICC must be directly engaged by external actors where circumstances so warrant it. Constructive UN Security Council engagement with the Court can only enhance and consolidate its reputation and, in turn, its deterrent effect. And constant, swift and firm reminders by both governmental and non-governmental sources to 'vulnerable constituencies' of the serious *personal* legal implications and ramifications of any actions they may be contemplating or have just embarked upon, remain an essential component in this mix. In practical terms, this could take the form of rapid deployment missions by prominent politicians to affected countries/regions. And, in parallel, ICC outreach and technical assistance programmes must continue undiminished. Information is power.

Success in Curbing Genocide

While it is premature to make any definitive assessment regarding the ICC's deterrent effect in respect of the future commission or restraint from commission of genocide, crimes against humanity or war crimes, early indications are promising:

- At a public hearing with the ICC Prosecutor in June 2003, Antoine Bernard, President of the International Federation of Human Rights (FIDH) observed that swift action by FIDH and media broadcasts in the Central African Republic (CAR) following a coup attempt in October 2002 reportedly led to a reduction in tension of the situation, which highlighted the possibility of a referral to the ICC, reportedly led to a reduction in tension of the situation (according to FIDH and other local NGO [nongovernmental organization] sources on the ground). In particular, a communiqué calling for ICC intervention that was widely broadcasted on national and international radios became a key factor in the decision of the main belligerent to move out from the country with his armed followers. In this respect, it must be noted that the alleged crimes in question fall under the jurisdiction of the ICC, as the Rome Statute entered into force on July 1, 2002, and the crimes were allegedly committed in October 2002. This action undertaken by civil society was reinforced by the decision of the Government of the CAR to refer their country-situation to the ICC on December 21, 2004—in fact, the referral requests the ICC Prosecutor to investigate any crime committed after July 1, 2002. The Prosecutor is currently analysing and closely monitoring the situation.

- The UN News Service reported on November 17, 2004, on comments made by the UN Operation in Côte d'Ivoire (UNOCI) that, a day after UN Special Advisor on Genocide Juan Mendez remarked that the situation in Côte d'Ivoire was falling under the jurisdiction of the ICC, *"National Radio and Television have been airing peace messages significantly different in tone and content to the ones we have been hearing of late"*. On November 16, Mr. Juan Mendez had said: *"The Special Adviser recalls that the Ivoirian authorities have an obligation to end impunity and to curb public expressions of racial or religious hatred especially those aimed at inciting violence. It should be recalled that, in the absence of effective action by courts of national jurisdiction, incitement to violence directed against civilians or ethnic, religious or racial communities can be subject to international action, including under the Rome Statute of the International Criminal Court. For instance, the Security Council could refer the situation in Cote d'Ivoire to the International Criminal Court. It bears noting that Cote d'Ivoire lodged a declaration with the Registrar accepting the exercise of jurisdiction by the International Criminal*

Court with respect to 'acts committed on Ivoirian territory following the events of 19 September 2002.' It would be very important for PGA and its membership to take stock of the effectiveness of Mr. Mendez's message and similarly utilize the *threat* of ICC intervention to curb the violence and break the cycle of impunity in other future situations, when and if the circumstances would appear to justify such an intervention.

- The most remarkable achievement of the initial practise of the ICC has been, so far, its fundamental contribution to the suspension of hostilities in Northern Uganda. As noted by the Representative of the High Commissioner for Human Rights In Kampala at a Panel Discussion in Kampala in September 2006, and as recently confirmed by statements of the US Ambassador to Uganda reproduced in the media, "peace-talks" between the Lord's Resistance Army (LRA) and the Ugandan Government would have not resumed with serious prospects of success without the arrest warrants issued by the ICC in July 2005 against Joseph Kony and 4 other leaders of the LRA. In June 2006, a top official of the UN Department of Peacekeeping Operations (DPKO) and a senior South African diplomat to the PGA's Director of Programmes at the UN that "Kony is terrorised by the prospect of being arrested and surrendered to the ICC!" An agreement between the ICC Prosecutor and the Government of Sudan to enforce the arrest warrants further weakened the position of the LRA leadership, who found refuge across the border of the Democratic Republic of Congo (in the Garanga National Park). "*As a consequence, crimes allegedly committed by the LRA in Northern Uganda have dramatically decreased*", Prosecutor Luis Moreno Ocampo stated in his address to the V Assembly of States Parties to the ICC in The Hague on November 23, 2006. He added:

"*People are leaving the camps for displaced persons, and the night commuter shelters which protected tens of thousands of children are in the process of closing. The loss of their safe haven led the LRA commanders to engage in negotiations, resulting in a cessation of hostilities agreement in August 2006.*" As of today, these events attest the deterrent impact of the ICC intervention, as no LRA attack against civilians has been reported over the past months after almost 20 years of armed conflict in Northern Uganda.

In all current or future crisis situations, Parliamentarians—as political leaders—may make their best efforts to disseminate knowledge of the Rome Statute and the implications for would-be perpetrators of ICC jurisdiction in connection with their present and future criminal plans and actions. Additionally, Parliamentarians could urge all relevant national, regional and international actors, such as the United Nations, the European Union and the African Union, to alert political and military leaders regarding the implications of ICC potential jurisdiction over their actions. In so doing, Parliamentarians will be able to contribute to this pivotal preventative function of the ICC.

Coordinated and concerted actions by all relevant actors in the next few years, as outlined above, should lay the groundwork for the ICC to assume its indisputably most important role—that as a force of deterrence.

The International Criminal Court Faces Obstacles in Preventing Future Genocides

Ian Black

Ian Black is a foreign affairs columnist for the Guardian *newspaper in Manchester, England. In the following article, Black describes the various obstacles the International Criminal Court (ICC) faces in meting out justice in cases of genocide, war crimes, and crimes against humanity. Chief among these is the refusal of the United States, China, Russia, and India to join the court. Black states that the ICC is also hampered by its inability to widely exercise its jurisdiction, being limited only to crimes committed by nationals of member states.*

Under the watchful eyes of [UN secretary-general] Kofi Annan and the Queen of the Netherlands, 18 judges [were] sworn in [on March 11, 2003,] as the most important human rights institution the world has seen in half a century [was] formally inaugurated.

The ceremony in the Dutch parliament marks the coming of age for the international criminal court [ICC]—and the fulfilment of a dream that began with the Nuremberg and Tokyo tribunals for Nazi and Japanese war criminals, and later found expression in the work of the UN tribunals for the former Yugoslavia and Rwanda.

But the ICC will be a new and, crucially, a permanent feature of the geopolitical landscape. It faces enormous challenges, including powerful American opposition, the task of choosing a prosecutor—and deciding who to put in the dock.

Ian Black, "International Criminal Court Comes to Life: Justice for Genocide Victims Now in Sight but American Opposition Threatens to Hamstring New Institution," *The Guardian* (London, England), March 11, 2003. Copyright 2003 Guardian Newspapers Limited. Reproduced by permission of Guardian News Service, Ltd.

Bringing Genocide to Justice

The court's job is to provide justice for genocide, crimes against humanity and war crimes, so that future victims have somewhere to turn to when national systems fail.

Bruno Cathala, the French judge who has been overseeing the ICC since it came into existence [in the summer of 2002], can hardly contain his excitement. "This is about globalised justice," he said. "No one has ever built an international criminal court before. We are going to fill the impunity gap."

Getting this far has been a long haul. The US, China, Russia and India remain opposed. Neither Iraq nor Israel has signed up. And Washington continues to pick off small countries to sign deals ensuring that American personnel are guaranteed immunity.

But 89 other states now back the court, and the moment is approaching when the first pre-trial investigation will be launched: its likely target is the Congolese rebel leader Jean-Pierre Bemba.

Still an Abstract Concept

The Bemba case falls into the category of those where a "state party" to the ICC statute—in this case the Democratic Republic of Congo—is either "unwilling or unable" to prosecute a suspected war criminal.

"At the moment the ICC is a highly abstract concept, and it can only start to be real when it gets its teeth into actual cases," said Steve Crawshaw, of Human Rights Watch.

"That's when it will start to be a highly important player on the world stage."

Before that, though, a prosecutor must be found. "His or her decisions will have a crucial impact on the court's development and credibility," says the Dutch government, an enthusiastic supporter. "It is vital to find someone whose credentials are impeccable."

This is proving difficult. Richard Goldstone, the first prosecutor at the Yugoslav tribunal, does not intend to leave his native South Africa. Carla del Ponte, the current incumbent, wants to see the [Yugoslav leader Slobodan] Milosevic case through. Other top candidates are holding back.

High politics and great sensitivities are at work here: the judges' bitterly fought election produced seven women and 11 men from Africa, Asia, the Caribbean, eastern Europe, Latin America, North America, and western Europe.

"We would not like to see this court becoming a court to prosecute poor countries or just Africa," warned the South African judge Navanethem Pillay, who is the president of the Rwanda tribunal.

Staff numbers are to jump from 40 to 200 by the end of [2003], but a big concern is to avoid creating a bloated and costly bureaucracy. "We need a 'plug-and-play' court that we can take anywhere in the world so that we don't have to bring everyone to the Hague," explains said Mr Cathala, the former deputy registrar of the Yugoslav tribunal.

"We are not trying to create a judicial empire here; quite the opposite," said Mr Cathala. "Paradoxically, one measure of our success will be not doing too much."

Obstacles to Success

Under the principle that the ICC will serve only as a court of "last resort", other cases are likely to be generated by the conflicts in Colombia and Sierra Leone.

Since jurisdiction is not retroactive, crimes committed before July [2002] cannot be tried.

No one claims the court will be perfect. Final negotiations saw its statute weakened, so it can try only crimes committed by nationals of governments that ratify the treaty, or in the territories of ratifying states.

Some also doubt that its ambitions can be realised as long as the US stays out. Washington insists it is not trying to undermine the court, just to protect US personnel abroad from an "unaccountable" prosecutor. Russian actions in Chechnya, like Israel's in the occupied Palestinian territories, will also be off limits for the foreseeable future, risking accusations of selective justice. . . .

No wonder then, despite Mr Cathala's optimism and the likelihood that more countries will eventually join, that the future looks so uncertain.

"The ICC is likely to survive, but without the US and other key countries it is unlikely to be very significant," a leading American legal expert said.

Remembering the Jewish Holocaust Can Prevent Future Genocides

Irwin Cotler

Irwin Cotler is a Canadian Member of Parliament and an international human rights lawyer. In the following transcript of his speech given at the Holocaust commemoration ceremony at the United Nations European headquarters, Cotler summarizes the universal lessons of the Holocaust, beginning with the importance of remembrance. Cotler emphasizes the responsibilities that must be accepted today to guard against such a tragedy ever happening again. These responsibilities include the duty to educate all people of the importance of Holocaust remembrance and the duty to always protect the most vulnerable members of society.

May I now summarize the universal lessons of the Holocaust—the lessons to be learned and the action to be taken. For as [Danish philosopher Soren] Kierkegaard put it, "life must be lived forwards, but it can only be understood backwards".

Lesson 1—The Importance of Holocaust Remembrance

The first lesson is the importance of *Zachor*, of remembrance itself. For as we remember the six million Jewish victims of the Shoah [the Hebrew term for the Holocaust]—defamed, demonized and dehumanized, as prologue or justification for genocide—we have to understand that the mass murder of six million Jews and millions of non-Jews is not a matter of abstract statistics.

Irwin Cotler, "Holocaust Remembrance," keynote address given at United Nations European headquarters, Geneva, Switzerland, January 29, 2007. www.irwincotler.parl .gc.ca. Reproduced by permission of Irwin Cotler.

For unto each person there is a name—unto each person, there is an identity. Each person is a universe. As our sages tell us: "whoever saves a single life, it is as if he or she has saved an entire universe." Just as whoever has killed a single person, it is as if they have killed an entire universe. And so the abiding imperative—that we are each, wherever we are, the guarantors of each other's destiny.

Lesson 2—The Responsibility to Prevent

The enduring lesson of the Holocaust is that the genocide of European Jewry succeeded not only because of the industry of death and the technology of terror, but because of the state-sanctioned ideology of hate. This teaching of contempt, this demonizing of the other, this is where it all began. As the Canadian courts affirmed in upholding the constitutionality of anti-hate legislation, "the Holocaust did not begin in the gas chambers—it began with words". These, as the Courts put it, are the chilling facts of history. These are the catastrophic effects of racism.

Forty years later, in the Nineties, these lessons not only remained unlearned, but the tragedy was repeated. For we witnessed, yet again, a growing trafficking in state-sanctioned hate and incitement, which in the Balkans and in Rwanda took us down the road to genocide.

And as we meet, we are witnessing yet again, a state-sanctioned incitement to hate and genocide, whose epicentre is [President Mahmoud] Ahmadinejad's Iran—and I distinguish President Ahmadinejad from the people of Iran, many of whom have themselves repudiated his remarks. For President Ahmadinejad denies the Nazi Holocaust as he incites to a Middle Eastern one—an assault on Jewish memory and truth in its denial of the Holocaust, which the U.N. General Assembly rebuked [in early 2007]; and a violation of the prohibition against the "direct and public incitement to genocide" in the Genocide Convention, which U.N. Secretaries-General Kofi

Annan and Ban Ki-Moon respectively called "shocking" and "unacceptable", indeed, an assault on the very U.N. charter, which prohibits such incitement and threat.

Lesson 3—The Duty to Protect

The genocide of European Jewry succeeded not only because of the state-sanctioned culture of hate and industry of death, but because of crimes of indifference, because of conspiracies of silence.

We meet today in the majestic Salle des Assemblées of the former League of Nations. It was here that Ethiopian Emperor Haile Selassie pleaded in vain for protection from Mussolini's 1935 aggression. Fascism marched ahead, winning one victory after another. It was here that while the gathering storm of war advanced, with Czechoslovakia surrendering to Hitler in 1938, further appeals for protection went unheeded. The response was international indifference, a failure of moral resolve, and the result was world war and genocide.

We are assembled here on the banks of Lake Geneva, on the other side of which lies Evian-des-Bains. It was here in 1938 that the international community considered the plight of hundreds of thousands of Jewish refugees desperate to flee worsening persecutions in Nazi Germany and Austria. But the nations looked away. As it was said at the time, the world was divided into those places where the Jews could not live, and those places where they could not enter. Hitler drew his lessons.

As we gather here today to commemorate the Holocaust in this historic Assembly Hall, with the representatives of the international community and civil society, let us pledge that never again will we be indifferent to aggression, hatred and incitement.

And indeed we have witnessed an appalling indifference and inaction in our own day which took us down the road to the unthinkable—ethnic cleansing in the Balkans—and down the road to the unspeakable—the genocide in Rwanda—unspeakable because this genocide was preventable. No one can say that we did not know. We knew, but we did not act, just as we know and have yet to act to stop the genocide by attrition in Darfur, ignoring the lessons of history, betraying the people of Darfur, and mocking the Responsibility to Protect doctrine [of the United Nations].

And so, it is our responsibility to break down these walls of indifference, to shatter these conspiracies of silence and inaction—to stand up and be counted and not look around to see whoever else is standing before we make a judgement to do so; because in the world in which we live, there are few enough people prepared to stand, let alone be counted, reminding us of the words of [philosopher] Edmund Burke, "the surest way to ensure that evil will triumph in the world is for enough good people to do nothing".

Indifference and inaction always mean coming down on the side of the victimizer, never on the side of the victim. Let there be no mistake about it—indifference in the face of evil is acquiescence with evil itself—it is complicity with evil.

Lesson 4—The Responsibility to Bring War Criminals to Justice

If the 20th Century—symbolized by the Holocaust—was the age of atrocity, it was also the age of impunity. Few of the perpetrators were brought to justice; and so, just as there must be no sanctuary for hate, no refuge for bigotry, there must be no base or sanctuary for these enemies of humankind. In this context, the establishment of the International Criminal Court must be seen as the most dramatic development in international criminal law since [the Nazi war crimes trials at] Nuremberg—to deter mass atrocity, to protect the victims, and to prosecute the perpetrators.

Lesson 5—The Responsibility to Talk Truth to Power

The Holocaust was made possible, not only because of the "bureaucratization of genocide", as [American psychiatrist] Robert Lifton put it, but because of the *trahison des clercs*— the complicity of the elites—physicians, church leaders, judges, lawyers, engineers, architects, educators, and the like. Indeed, one only has to read Gerhard Muller's book on "Hitler's Justice" to appreciate the complicity and criminality of judges and lawyers; or to read Robert-Jan van Pelt's book on the architecture of Auschwitz, to be appalled by the minute involvement of engineers and architects in the design of death camps, and so on. Holocaust crimes, then, were also the crimes of the Nuremberg elites. As [Holocaust survivor, author, and political activist] Elie Wiesel put it, "Cold-blooded murder and culture did not exclude each other. If the Holocaust proved anything, it is that a person can both love poems and kill children".

And so it is our responsibility to speak truth to power, and to hold power accountable to truth. And those entrusted with the education and training of the elites should ensure that Elie Wiesel is studied in schools of law and not just in classes of literature; that the double entendre of Nuremberg—of Nuremberg racism as well as the Nuremberg Principles—is part of our learning as it is part of our legacy; that Holocaust education underpin our perspective as it informs our principles—on justice and injustice.

Lesson 6—The Responsibility to Educate

Sweden is a case-study of how Holocaust education, can not only teach an entire society of the importance of Holocaust remembrance and reminder—of witness and warning—but how it can engage that whole society in "living history"—in the teaching, learning, and internalization of Holocaust sensibility—where the particularity of the Holocaust has universal resonance.

In particular, in the spirit of the International Day of Commemoration in Memory of the Victims of the Holocaust, states should commit themselves to the constituent elements of the Declaration of the Stockholm International Forum on the Holocaust, which included ... the understanding that:

> the Holocaust fundamentally challenged the foundations of civilization ... [its] unprecedented character will always hold universal meaning ... [its] magnitude ... must be forever seared in our collective memory ... together we must uphold the terrible truths of the Holocaust against those who deny it.
>
> We must strengthen the moral commitment of our people and the political commitment of our governments, to ensure that future generations can understand the causes of the Holocaust and reflect upon its consequences.
>
> We pledge to strengthen efforts to promote education, remembrance and research about the Holocaust. ...
>
> We share a commitment to encourage the study of the Holocaust in all its dimensions ... a commitment to commemorate the victims of the Holocaust and to honour those who stood against it ... a commitment to throw light on the still obscured shadows of the Holocaust ... a commitment to plant the seeds of a better future amidst the soil of a bitter past ... a commitment ... to remember the victims who perished, respect the survivors still with us, and reaffirm humanity's common aspiration for mutual understanding and justice.

Lesson 7—The Protection of the Vulnerable as the Test of a Just Society

The genocide of European Jewry occurred not only because of the vulnerability of the powerless, but also because of the powerlessness of the vulnerable. It is not surprising that the triage of Nazi racial hygiene—the Sterilization Laws, the

Nuremberg Race Laws, the Euthanasia Program—targeted those "whose lives were not worth living"; and it is not unrevealing, as Professor Henry Friedlander points out in his work on "The Origins of Genocide", that the first group targeted for killing were the Jewish disabled—the whole anchored in the science of death, the medicalization of ethnic cleansing, the sanitizing even of the vocabulary of destruction.

And so it is our responsibility as government representatives . . . to give voice to the voiceless, as we seek to empower the powerless—be they the disabled, the poor, the refugee, the elderly, the women victims of violence, the vulnerable child—the most vulnerable of the vulnerable. . . .

A Commitment to Action

We remember—and we pledge—and this must not be a matter of rhetoric but must be a commitment to action—that never again will we be indifferent to incitement and hate; that never again will we be silent in the face of evil; that never again will we indulge racism and anti-Semitism; that never again will we ignore the plight of the vulnerable; that never again will we be indifferent in the face of mass atrocity and impunity.

We will speak and we will act against racism, against hate, against anti-Semitism, against mass atrocity, against injustice—and against the crime of crimes whose name we should even shudder to mention—genocide.

And yes, always, against indifference, against being bystanders to injustice. For in what we say, or more importantly in what we do, we will be making a statement about ourselves as a people, we will be making a statement about ourselves as people. For in our day, more than ever, . . . whoever remains indifferent indicts themselves.

May this day be not only an act of remembrance, which it is, but let it be a remembrance to act, which it must be.

Remembering the Jewish Holocaust Cannot Prevent Future Genocides

Paul Treanor

In the following viewpoint Paul Treanor, a Netherlands-based political science writer, argues that the Jewish holocaust must be forgotten. He asserts that the memory of the Holocaust is used by politicians to justify acts of warfare on other countries. Ultimately, Treanor concludes that memories of the Holocaust are used to legitimize injustices rather than prevent the occurrence of future genocides.

At least until 11 September 2001, the Holocaust was the primary historical reference used to justify military intervention, by the US and its allies. Indirectly, it is also used to legitimise social injustice in liberal-democratic nations, and to imply a liberal-democratic entitlement to a monopoly of power. It is used to legitimise global inequality, as if it entitled opponents of the Holocaust to prosperity, while others starve. Remembering the Holocaust is not a moral imperative: the memory serves no good purpose, only evil purposes. The Holocaust should be publicly forgotten, in the same sense as it is now publicly remembered. . . .

Selective Remembrance

In how far is knowledge of atrocities a deliberate decision, in the the real political culture of western nations? The fact that governments publicly appeal to atrocity stories to justify their actions, draws increased attention to them. Aside from that, government and military organisations do specifically publi-

Paul Treanor, "Why Forget the Holocaust?" February 2007. http://web.inter.nl.net/users/ Paul.Treanor/forget.html. Reproduced by permission.

cise them: during the Kosovo war, the daily NATO press conferences were also the daily atrocity reports. The media also report independently on atrocities, and in turn this material is used by governments. The distinction between war reporting, propaganda and espionage—always unclear—almost disappeared during the Kosovo war.

The best evidence, that the public knowledge of atrocities is the result of deliberate action, is its selectivity. If it were simply a case of western media reporting human suffering, the public would know as much about the war in southern Sudan, as they knew about Kosovo. (If and when it suits the aims of western governments, then they will see that war nightly on their TV screens.) Knowledge of past atrocities is equally selective. The western public does know about the Killing Fields of Cambodia: the use of the film title indicates *why* they know. Without the film, Cambodia would have retained the status it had in another title: a book on the US war on Cambodia is titled "Sideshow".

A more interesting comparison is with the Belgian exploitation of the Congo (in fact by a private enterprise owned by the Belgian Royal Family). Outside Belgium, the scale of this atrocity is unknown: possibly more people died as a result of harsh treatment during the initial decades of colonisation, than died in the Holocaust. In general it is not 'remembered', because so few people set out to remember it. No movie, no memory. Public memory is as politicised, and as selective, as public knowledge of present atrocities. It is a result of decisions about what to remember, and in what form. Perhaps the most extraordinary illustration of the selectiveness of memory is the 'Armenian genocide', by Ottoman forces during the First World War. Europe forgot the Armenians, until after the Second World War a comment by Hitler on the fate of the Jews became famous. "Who remembers the Armenians?" asked Hitler. And because Hitler asked, and because of the historical status of both Hitler and the Holocaust, the Armenians are now remembered. (In turn, that memorialisation became a political issue, with consequences for Turkey's accession to the European Union.)

There is no comparison between public memory and individual memory, just as there is no comparison between public and private knowledge of atrocities. A person who has been in a concentration camp can not make decisions about whether to remember it. If you see a mass killing, then you know about it, and you will never forget it. Yet societies, as the examples show, *can* be selective. Therefore, they can be deliberate. There is a decision to know, and a decision to remember.

There are still a few people alive, with personal memory of the Holocaust, just as there are people who saw atrocities in Kosovo. But no moral duty to public memory follows from that fact. If that public memory causes harm to innocent third parties, then it is better that they be silent—or even deny their own suffering. . . .

Real-world decisions on memory can not be taken as if in a vacuum. It is not an absolute wrong to forget the Holocaust: there can be ethical grounds to do so. Just as its memory has been preserved by deliberate decisions, to build Holocaust museums and memorials, these decisions can be reversed. It can be ethically legitimate to do this. Yet until now, all the decisions have been decisions to remember—partly because no-one presents the option of forgetting.

Political Uses

So what is done with the memory that has been decided upon? As an almost universal symbol of evil, the Holocaust is widely used for political purposes. . . . What people do not like, or seek to destroy, they compare to the Holocaust. Evangelical Christians, for instance, see it as a warning against the occult, and against the loss of Christian values. Some post-modernists saw it as a revelation of the logic of modernity. Right-wing-

historians in Germany tried to blame it on the left, by claiming the Nazi regime imitated the Soviet Union.

The Holocaust has two more directly political uses. The first is the affirmation of liberal-democratic societies, by reference to the Holocaust. Often this is combined with a claim that a specific nation (Britain, Canada, the United States, Australia) helped to end it. The other political use is during international conflict: the accusation that opponents are "like the Nazis", that their actions are "like the Holocaust"—and "therefore" that retaliatory action is justified. A long list of anti-western leaders have been compared to Adolf Hitler: in return, many of them said the same thing about western leaders. But only in the last 20 years, has the Holocaust acquired its present force in the politics of western liberal-democratic states. Reference to the Holocaust now signals imminent military action. . . .

The appeal to the Holocaust plays an important role in 'democratic expansionism'. Supporters of democracy used to say that democracies were good because they did not engage in wars of conquest. Today, the consensus in western democracies is, that they *should* go to war—to bring their values to the rest of the world. A few countries (Switzerland, Britain, the United States) developed democracy themselves, but most democracies have democratic systems because they were invaded or colonised by democratic states. The most recent 'democratisations'—Iraq above all—are among the most violent in history.

For at least a century, some people have proposed that democratic states should join forces, to conquer the rest of the world. They had little support at first, but by now this idea has ceased to be marginal. Even before the rise of the neoconservative policy advisors in Washington, a school of intervention ethics emerged in the western foreign-policy elites, and in English-language moral philosophy. The Holocaust was its historical reference point. Few people simply argue that "because of the Holocaust, the US should conquer the world". However, as the US and its allies increasingly intervene to create 'democratising protectorates', the historical reference is used case-by-case. The case of Kosovo is exemplary: the NATO/OSCE [Organization for Security and Cooperation in Europe] intervention had the explicit aim of remodelling society, as well as ending atrocities. (Kosovo will continue to be a semi-protectorate of the European Union under the latest proposals, the 2007 Ahtisaari plan.) The intervention in Kosovo was explicitly and repeatedly legitimised by reference to the Holocaust. . . .

The 2003 invasion of Iraq was officially intended to remove weapons of mass destruction, but in reality it was inspired by an aggressive interventionist ideology. President [George W.] Bush later invoked the Holocaust as a justification for its crusading aspect. The war in Iraq, according to President Bush, is inseparable from a wider crusade against the Holocaust. Speaking after a visit to the [Nazi concentration] camp at Auschwitz-Birkenau, he said it was a reminder that "evil must be opposed". In case anyone is in doubt what that means, in the same speech he also threatened North Korea with a naval blockade. New wars are coming, to defeat more 'new Hitlers'.

In a less explicit way, liberal-democratic societies are partly founded on Holocaust memory. In theory, liberal social philosophy is 'non-foundational'—it does not start from some principle of what society ought to be. In practice, the liberal social model presents itself as an alternative to the horrors of war, poverty and dictatorship—the *only* alternative.

In Germany this foundationalism is at its most explicit. The German state, and the German social elite, constantly refer to Nazi Germany as legitimation of their own political existence. In turn, any deviance from official democratic orthodoxy is at once attacked, as an imminent return to the Nazi era. The great emphasis in Germany on the evil of the Nazi regime is often misunderstood as a sign of guilt: in fact it is more a self-congratulation of present Germany, for being so different. The curious way in which the German army honours [Claus] von Stauffenberg (the man who almost killed Hitler) is typical. Armies do not normally honour officers who try to assassinate the nation's leader in wartime. But in this way, the German army is retroactively on the winning side, the liberal-democratic side, the anti-Holocaust side.

The Holocaust plays an increasing role in this form of national legitimation. Public atonement by German politicians may have a completely different meaning for them, than for their foreign audience. In Germany, the Holocaust is being transformed from a symbol of national shame to a symbol of national pride. . . .

The late construction of a Holocaust memorial in Berlin (something never imposed on the city by the occupying allies), should be seen in this light. And if the Holocaust can be used in this way in Germany, how much easier to do that in countries whose troops *liberated* concentration camps. That is one reason why there is a large National Holocaust Museum in Washington. That is one explanation for the status of [teenage author] Anne Frank as national symbol of the Netherlands. There is an *implicit foundational mythology for liberal societies*—an 'Auschwitz myth' in an accurate sense of the word. It is not in fact their historical foundation—in reality liberalism and liberal-democracy existed before Auschwitz—and it is not transparent or explicit. This vague mythology implies that the Holocaust is the negation of liberal society, and that liberal society is consequently the negation of the Holocaust, the remedy for it—the appropriate historical 'fire extinguisher'. It suggests that the Holocaust was caused by the lack of liberalism—by failure to meet something like the Freedom House checklist of liberal-democratic rights. It also implies that liberal democracy ended the Holocaust. That last claim is 'mythological' in the sense of false: most concentration camps, including Auschwitz itself, were in eastern Europe, and were liberated by Soviet troops.

The Elite and Holocaust Memory

The ethics of this use of memory are simple: it is wrong to legitimise a society which is wrong. And there are many things wrong with the nation state, and with liberal-democratic societies in general. One relevant characteristic in this context, is that most liberal-democratic theorists believe in the inherent inequality of the talented and the untalented. Liberal-democratic societies are characterised by social inequality generated by competition. It is apparently the inevitable outcome of liberal process, and liberals believe that process justifies outcome. If there were no Holocaust to remember, indeed if all historical atrocities were forgotten without trace, liberal-democratic societies would not instantly collapse. But the self-congratulatory attitude that Holocaust memory promotes—"our society is the best in history"—is certainly an obstacle to innovation and justice in that society. . . .

And certainly, the elite, in western societies, does not hesitate to accuse the opposition of being 'like the Nazis'. As with the Holocaust comparisons in international crises, this does have effects. It protects the social order against radical change. (It does not work the other way around: as millions of demonstrators have discovered, shouting "Fascists!" at the police does not make them disappear.)

So it is no surprise, that those who want to remember the Holocaust are the elite, the privileged, the holders of power. Institutions of Holocaust memory are 'white' and 'middle-class'. Apart from the survivors of the Holocaust itself, the memorialists are predominantly the members of the ethnic majority in each nation, people with an income and educational level well above average. The poorest people in the world devote no energy to memorialising the Holocaust.

Is any good done by Holocaust memory? It clearly has effects, and some people value these effects. One response to my views was that Holocaust memory at least brought justice for the surviving victims, and that it gave people a capacity to judge the present in terms of the past and an "awareness of the magnitude of modern human cruelty". But that is the problem: much modern human cruelty is legitimised by historical reference to the Holocaust. The ethics of Holocaust memory repeatedly refer to utilitarian arguments: about sacrificing one to save many. . . .

The truth is that the memory of the Holocaust does not incite people to do absolute and unconditional good. It usually serves to justify harm to others. I have never seen any postwar example where the Holocaust inspired a person to act in an unquestionably good way. I see many examples where people do things they know are controversial—and quote the Holocaust in defence of their actions. The more extreme the actions, the more likely they are to appeal to the Holocaust.

Remembering the Holocaust is like placing a live hand grenade in a room full of small children. It is no good to them in any way, and sooner or later they will play with it, and kill or injure themselves. Only an evil person would do such a thing. Those who place Holocaust memory on earth are the historians, the archivists, the museum directors, the writers, the designers of Holocaust memorials, the creators of memory websites. Politicians and philosophers demand and emphasise Holocaust memory. They bear a heavy responsibility, and it is increasing. A hypothetical United States conquest of Africa, to "implement human rights and stop genocide", would probably kill over ten million people. (That guess is based on the civilian deaths in Iraq and Vietnam.) The longer the Holocaust is remembered, the more people will suffer, the more people will die, the more injustice will be done—all with reference to that memory. The right thing to do is to terminate the memory.

Organizations to Contact

The editors have compiled the following list of organizations concerned with the issues debated in this book. The descriptions are derived from materials provided by the organizations. All have publications or information available for interested readers. The list was compiled on the date of publication of the present volume; the information provided here may change. Be aware that many organizations take several weeks or longer to respond to inquiries, so allow as much time as possible.

Amnesty International (AI)
5 Penn Plaza, 14th Floor, New York, NY   10001
(212) 807-8400 • fax: (212) 463-9193
e-mail: admin-us@aiusa.org
Web site: www.amnestyusa.org

AI is a worldwide movement of people who campaign for internationally recognized human rights. By providing articles, publications, pamphlets, and video media, AI seeks to educate people about all human rights violations and call people to action. AI prints regular reports, such as *Human Rights for Human Dignity: A Primer on Economic, Social and Cultural Rights* and *"Disappearances" and Political Killings: A Manual for Action* by both a country-by-country basis as well as a thematic basis.

Armenian American Society for Studies on Stress and Genocide (AASSSG)
139 Cedar St., Cliffside Park, NJ   07010
(201) 941-2266 • fax: (201) 941-5110
e-mail: akalayjian@meaningfulworld.com
Web site: www.meaningfulworld.com

Established in 1988, AASSSG is dedicated to the scientific study of the stresses of genocide and other mass traumas. More specifically, its goal is to advance national and international understanding of the generational and intergenerational effects of such traumatic experiences. In addition to annual conferences, the AASSSG regularly publishes reports and scholarly research focused on the aftermath of genocide and genocide prevention, including the *General Impact of Mass Trauma: The Post-Ottoman Turkish Genocide of the Armenians.*

Cambodian Genocide Program (CGP)

PO Box 208206, New Haven, CT   06520-8206
e-mail: cgp@yale.edu
Web site: www.yale.edu/cgp

Since 1994, the Yale University–based CGP has been collecting and archiving documentation of the Cambodian genocide in an effort to find whom among Pol Pot's regime was responsible. The efforts of the CGP lie primarily in collecting and translating the original documents and making them available for study. In addition, the members continually publish and present papers, articles, and books, such as Ben Kiernan's "Bringing the Khmer Rouge to Justice," in *Human Rights Review,* or the book *Cambodia* (World Bibliographical Series) by Helen Jarvis.

Coalition Against Genocide (CAG)

8480 Baltimore National Pike, #286
Ellicott City, MD   21043
tel/fax: (443) 927-9039
e-mail: info@coalitionagainstgenocide.org
Web site: www.coalitionagainstgenocide.org

The Coalition Against Genocide is an organization of both groups and individuals established to combat genocide and bring the perpetrators of genocide to justice. CAG was formed after the 2002 violence in Gujarat, India, in the belief that it was an act of genocide against Muslim peoples, and that those responsible walk free. By distributing posters and providing documentaries, the group hopes to raise awareness and promote international action.

Facing History and Ourselves National Foundation (FHAO)

16 Hurd Rd., Brookline, MA   02445-6919
(617) 232-1595 • fax: (617) 232-0281
Web site: www.facinghistory.org

Since 1976, FHAO has been engaging students of diverse backgrounds in an examination of racism, prejudice, and anti-Semitism in order to promote the development of a more humane and informed citizenry. By studying the historical development and lessons of the Holocaust and other examples of genocide, students make the essential connection between history and the choices they confront in their own lives. In addition to offering online classes to educators and students, FHAO regularly produces resource books and study guides, including *I'm Still Here: Real Diaries of Young People During the Holocaust, Crimes Against Humanity and Civilization: The Genocide of the Armenians,* and *The Jews of Poland.*

Genocide Intervention Network (GI-Net)

1333 H St. NW, Washington, DC   20005
(202) 481-8220
e-mail: info@genocideintervention.net
Web site: www.genocideintervention.net

GI-Net envisions a world in which the global community is willing and able to protect civilians from genocide and mass atrocities. In order to empower individuals and communities with the tools to prevent and stop genocide, GI-Net recommends activities from engaging government representatives to hosting fund-raisers. While maintaining many documents online regarding genocide, GI-Net provides an action plan to promote action as well as education.

Holocaust Resource Center (HRC) of Kean University

Kean University Library, 2nd Floor, Union, NJ   07083
(908) 737-4660 • fax: (908) 737-4664
e-mail: keanhrc@kean.edu
Web site: www.kean.edu/~hrc

The HRC of Kean University opened its doors in the fall semester of 1982. The center is a joint initiative between the university and the Holocaust Resource Foundation, a private philanthropic organization. The center collects and disseminates knowledge of the Holocaust to commemorate and strengthen education about the Holocaust. In addition, the center offers an annual free lecture series and a tuition-free graduate course for teachers called Teaching the Holocaust.

Institute for the Study of Genocide (ISG)
John Jay College of Criminal Justice, New York, NY   10019
e-mail info@isg-iags.org
Web site: www.isg-iags.org

The ISG is an independent nonprofit organization that exists to promote and disseminate scholarship and policy analyses on the causes, consequences, and prevention of genocide. To advance these ends, it publishes working papers and a semiannual newsletter; holds periodic conferences; maintains liaisons with academic, human rights, and refugee organizations; provides consultation to representatives of media, governmental and nongovernmental organizations; and advocates passage of legislation and administrative measures related to genocide and gross violations of human rights. The ISG also publishes books on the topic of genocide, such as *Ever Again? Evaluating the United Nations Genocide Convention on Its 50th Anniversary and Proposals to Activate the Convention* and *The Prevention of Genocide: Rwanda and Yugoslavia Reconsidered.*

International Association of Genocide Scholars (IAGS)
c/o Prof. Israel W. Charny, Ph.D., New York, NY   10019
tel/fax: +972-2-672-0424
e-mail: encygeno@mail.com
Web site: www.isg-iags.org

The IAGS is a global, interdisciplinary, nonpartisan organization that seeks to further research and education about the nature, causes, and consequences of genocide. The aim of the association is to focus more intensively on questions of genocide than is possible in the existing two-hour format of most conferences and to draw colleagues from different disciplines into an interdisciplinary conversation. The work at these conferences culminates in papers, newsletters, and books such as *Genocide: Essays Toward Understanding, Early Warning, and Prevention.*

Prevent Genocide International (PGI)

1804 S St. NW, Washington, DC   20009
(202) 483-1948 • fax (202) 328-0627
e-mail: info@preventgenocide.org
Web site: www.preventgenocide.org

PGI is a global education and action network established in 1998 with the purpose of bringing about the elimination of the crime of genocide. In an effort to promote education on the subject of genocide, PGI maintains a multilingual Web site both for the education of the international community as well as for the nations not yet belonging to the United Nations Genocide Convention in an effort to persuade these holdout countries. The Web site maintains a database of government documents and news releases as well as original content provided by members, such as Jim Fussell's *Group Classification on National ID Cards as a Factor in Genocide and Ethnic Cleansing,* presented to the Seminar Series of the Yale University Genocide Studies Program.

Student Anti-Genocide Coalition (STAND)

1333 H St., NW, Washington, DC   20005
(202) 481-8220
e-mail: info@standnow.org
Web site: www.standnow.org

Formerly Students Taking Action Now: Darfur, STAND now seeks a more general purpose of creating a permanent anti-genocide movement among students. While still seeking an end to violence in Darfur, Africa, STAND now promotes awareness of genocide through grassroots efforts of both high school and college students. Through its Web site, STAND provides educational materials, event planning, and media and press release how-to's.

United Human Rights Council (UHRC)
PO Box 10039, Glendale, CA   91206
(888)858-UHRC
Web site: www.unitedhumanrights.org

Formed to prevent governments from denying the violence in their pasts, the UHRC plans a more direct route to affecting countries with poor human rights records, including those that deny genocide. The UHRC plans campaigns of five years against violators in an effort to generate awareness and typically uses consumer boycotts to help rob the governments of revenues used to continue concealment efforts. The UHRC Web site focuses on the genocides of the twentieth century.

United States Holocaust Memorial Museum
100 Raoul Wallenberg Place SW
Washington, DC   20024-2126
(202) 488-0400 • TTY: (202) 488-0406
e-mail: ahollinger@ushmm.org
Web Site: www.ushmm.org

The goal of the United States Holocaust Museum is to document, study, and interpret Holocaust history, primarily that of the genocide during Nazi Germany, 1933–1945. By providing exhibits, maintaining lists of victims and survivors, and by providing a library and archives to visitors, the museum preserves the memories of the victims while provoking reflection on visitors' roles in preventing such actions again. The museum offers resources for both students and teachers on its Web site, as well as a series of online exhibitions, such as *Flight and Rescue* and *Life After the Holocaust*.

Bibliography

Books

Taner Akcam

A Shameful Act: The Armenian Genocide and the Question of Turkish Responsibility. New York: Metropolitan Books, 2006.

Michael J. Bazyler

Holocaust Justice: The Battle for Restitution in America's Courts. New York: New York University Press, 2003.

Donald Bloxham

The Great Game of Genocide: Imperialism, Nationalism and the Destruction of the Ottoman Armenians. New York: Oxford University Press, 2005.

Robert Gellately and Ben Kiernan, eds.

The Specter of Genocide: Mass Murder in Historical Perspective. New York: Cambridge University Press, 2003.

Neil Gregor, ed.

Nazism, War and Genocide: Essays in Honour of Jeremy Noakes. Exeter, UK: University of Exeter Press, 2005.

Jean Hatzfeld

Into the Quick of Life: The Rwandan Genocide: The Survivors Speak. London: Serpent's Tail, 2005.

Jean Hatzfeld

A Time for Machetes: The Rwandan Genocide: The Killers Speak. London: Serpent's Tail, 2005.

Immaculée Ilibagiza

Left to Tell: Discovering God Amidst the Rwandan Holocaust. New York: Hay House, 2006.

Hanna Jansen

Over a Thousand Hills I Walk with You. Minneapolis, MN: Carolrhoda Books, 2006.

Berel Lang

Post-Holocaust: Interpretation, Misinterpretation and the Claims of History. Bloomington: Indiana University Press, 2005.

Guenter Lewy

The Armenian Massacres in Ottoman Turkey: A Disputed Genocide. Salt Lake City: University of Utah Press, 2005.

Wendy Lower

Nazi Empire-Building and the Holocaust in Ukraine. Chapel Hill: University of North Carolina Press, 2005.

Michael Mann

The Dark Side of Democracy. Explaining Ethnic Cleansing. New York: Cambridge University Press, 2005.

Patricia Marchak

Reigns of Terror. Ithaca, NY: Queen's University Press, 2003.

Linda Melvern

Conspiracy to Murder: The Rwanda Genocide. New York: Verso, 2006.

Manus I. Midlarsky

The Killing Trap: Genocide in the Twentieth Century. New York: Cambridge University Press, 2005.

Kingsley Moghalu

Rwanda's Genocide: The Politics of Global Justice. New York: Palgrave Macmillan, 2005.

Thomas P. Odom

Journey into Darkness: Genocide in Rwanda. College Station: Texas A&M University Press, 2005.

Samantha Power	*A Problem from Hell: America and the Age of Genocide.* London: Flamingo, 2003.
Gérard Prunier	*Darfur: The Ambiguous Genocide.* Ithaca, NY: Cornell University Press, 2005.
Gretchen E. Schafft	*From Racism to Genocide: Anthropology in the Third Reich.* Urbana: University of Illinois Press, 2004.
Andrea Smith	*Conquest: Sexual Violence and American Indian Genocide.* Cambridge, MA: South End, 2005.
Scott Straus	*The Order of Genocide: Race, Power, and War in Rwanda.* Ithaca, NY: Cornell University Press, 2006.
John Lawrence Tone	*War and Genocide in Cuba, 1895–1898.* Chapel Hill: University of North Carolina Press, 2006.
Gilbert Tuhabonye and Gary Brozek	*This Voice in My Heart: A Genocide Survivor's Story of Escape, Faith, and Forgiveness.* New York: Amistad, 2006.
Benjamin A. Valentino	*Final Solutions: Mass Killing and Genocide in the Twentieth Century.* Ithaca, NY: Cornell University Press, 2004.
James Waller	*Becoming Evil: How Ordinary People Commit Genocide and Mass Killing.* New York: Oxford University Press, 2002.

Bruce Wilshire   *Get 'Em All! Kill 'Em!: Genocide, Ter-rorism, Righteous Communities.* Lan-ham, MD: Lexington Books, 2005.

Jay Winter, ed.   *America and the Armenian Genocide of 1915.* New York: Cambridge Uni-versity Press, 2003.

Periodicals

Armen   "Genocide Debate," *Wilson Quarterly*,
Baghdoyan   Spring 2006.

Peter Balakian   "Genocide?" *Commentary*, February 2006.

Rose Marie   "A Responsibility to Protect," *Sojourn-*
Berger   *ers*, December 2006.

Daniel S. Blocq   "The Fog of UN Peacekeeping: Ethi-cal Issues Regarding the Use of Force to Protect Civilians in UN Opera-tions," *Journal of Military Ethics*, No-vember 2006.

Gail Collins and   "Turkey, Armenia and Denial," *New*
Andrew Rosenthal   *York Times*, May 16, 2006.

Daniele Conversi   "Demo-Skepticism and Genocide," *Political Studies Review*, September 2006.

Alison Des Forges   "Origins of Rwandan Genocide," *Journal of African History*, 2005.

Ron Dudai	"Understanding Perpetrators in Genocides and Mass Atrocities," *British Journal of Sociology*, December 2006.
Roger Eatwell	"Explaining Fascism and Ethnic Cleansing: The Three Dimensions of Charisma and the Four Dark Sides of Nationalism," *Political Studies Review*, September 2006.
Geetanjali Gangoli	"Engendering Genocide: Gender, Conflict and Violence," *Women's Studies International Forum*, September 2006.
Yücel Güçlü	"Mislabeling Genocide?" *Middle East Quarterly*, Spring 2006.
Harper's Magazine	"Did Somebody Say Genocide?" August 2006.
Garin Hovannisian	"The Folly of Jailing Genocide Deniers," *Christian Science Monitor*, November 6, 2006.
Karen Kovach	"Genocide and the Moral Agency of Ethnic Groups," *Metaphilosophy*, July 2006.
Nicholas D. Kristof	"Why Genocide Matters," *New York Times*, September 9, 2006.
John Lasker	"Genocide Not Enough to Send in Troops?" *Black Enterprise*, October 2006.

Guillermo Levy — "Considerations on the Connections between Race, Politics, Economics, and Genocide," *Journal of Genocide Research*, June 2006.

Joseph Mussomeli — "'The Worst Genocide Ever,'" *Wall Street Journal*, August 1, 2006.

New Statesman — "Darfur: Lest We Forget (Again)," September 11, 2006.

Eric Reeves — "Watching Genocide, Doing Nothing," *Dissent*, Fall 2006.

Carlin Romano — "Is the Crematorium Half-Full or Half-Empty?" *Chronicle of Higher Education*, September 22, 2006.

Christine Stansell — "Torment and Justice in Cambodia," *Dissent*, Fall 2005.

Ervin Staub — "Reconciliation After Genocide, Mass Killing, or Intractable Conflict: Understanding the Roots of Violence, Psychological Recovery, and Steps Toward a General Theory," *Political Psychology*, December 2006.

Index